Highly
Successful
Women
Administrators

With love and admiration, I dedicate this book to my number-one role model in education and life, my dear mother, Eleanor.

—*Sandra Lee Gupton*

This book is dedicated in loving memory to my parents, Daisy Lea Guyon Appelt and Weldon Ferdinand Appelt. It is because of the modeling of their devotion and love for each other and for me that I love, respect, appreciate, and constantly strive to understand my fellow human beings as well as contribute whatever talents I may possess to the education profession.

I also wish to dedicate this book to Dr. G. Ray Musgrave, my lifelong professional mentor, whose belief in me made it possible for me to realize my potential as an educator.

—*Gloria Appelt Slick*

Highly Successful Women Administrators

The Inside Stories of How They Got There

Sandra Lee Gupton
Gloria Appelt Slick

CORWIN PRESS, INC.
A Sage Publications Company
Thousand Oaks, California

For information address:

Corwin Press, Inc.
A Sage Publications Company
2455 Teller Road
Thousand Oaks, California 91320
e-mail: order@corwin.sagepub.com

SAGE Publications Ltd.
6 Bonhill Street
London EC2A 4PU
United Kingdom

SAGE Publications India Pvt. Ltd.
M-32 Market
Greater Kailash I
New Delhi 110 048 India

Printed in the United States of America

Library of Congress Cataloging-in-Publication Data

Gupton, Sandra Lee.
    Highly successful women administrators: The inside stories of how they got there / authors, Sandra Lee Gupton, Gloria Appelt Slick.
      p. cm.
    Includes bibliographical references.
    ISBN 0-8039-6204-5 (acid-free paper). — ISBN 0-8039-6205-3 (pbk. : acid-free paper)
    1. Women school administrators—United States. 2. Women school administrators—Selection and appointment—United States. 3. Sex discrimination against women—United States. 4. Educational leadership—United States. I. Slick, Gloria Appelt. II. Title.
    LB2831.62.G87 1996
    371.2'0082—dc20   96-10120

This book is printed on acid-free paper.

96 97 98 99 00 10 9 8 7 6 5 4 3 2 1

Production Editor: Astrid Virding
Typesetter/Designer: Rebecca Evans/Tina Hill
Cover Designer: Marcia R. Finlayson

Contents

**CORWIN
PRESS**

The Corwin Press logo—a raven striding across an open book—
represents the happy union of courage and learning. We are a
professional-level publisher of books and journals for K–12 educators, and we are committed to creating and providing resources that
embody these qualities. Corwin's motto is "Success for All Learners."

Foreword

I wrote *Women Getting Together and Getting Ahead* with Joan Kalvelage and Mary Ann Smith more than a decade ago. It was a product of The Sex Equity in Educational Leadership Project, one of the first projects funded by the Women's Educational Equity Act in 1976. The book gives advice to women seeking leadership roles and is a comparative benchmark for *Education's Women Administrators*, which is an "up-to-date analysis of the evolution of issues underlying women's inequitable representation in executive positions in the profession." Comparing what we wrote earlier to the issues raised in 1996, things have not changed much. Gail, one of the storytellers in this book, says that women's status in educational administration has "changed a lot in some ways but not at all in others." I will expand on Gail's observation and focus on what has changed and what has not changed, what still remain as barriers to women's advancement and success, and what has changed for the better.

Citing the barriers, the 15 "wise and wonderful" women tell stories of family constraints, sex stereotypes, overt discrimination, differing social and job expectations based on gender, and self-struggle. Many of us probably will find their stories familiar.

— Catherine tells of putting off her own education to "put hubby through school" and then being divorced with a child to raise.

— Elizabeth relates how she made family sacrifices to serve her career.

— Gail tells of self-blame for events beyond her control.

— Marie and others give examples of overt discrimination in their university preparation programs with male professors and male-dominant texts.

— Emily and Brenda vividly describe the difficulties of being female in a leadership role and the different standards used to evaluate their performance.

— Emily is surprised that women faculty were not accepting of her leadership role and did not support her.

These disturbing narratives reflect also the survey data from 151 questionnaire respondents. The bad news is that 70% of women reported obstacles to their careers because they were women; 74% of women reported that they had negative role models—half of whom were women; and 57% said that they are not part of a network of professional support—even more disturbing is that 17% of these women said that they did not need or want such support. Gupton and Slick also point out that 20% of the respondents indicated that they have never been a mentor to others. Because there are so few female administrators, this is discouraging news. We cannot afford to lose the support and encouragement of the 20% of women administrators; they need to support and encourage others to become leaders. Indeed, there is a thread of antifeminism that runs through some of the narratives and some of the survey results. Some of these women want to deny their femaleness and seem to care only about their individual careers.

I find the antifeminist attitudes of some women administrators perplexing and have written about it elsewhere (Schmuck & Schubert, 1995). It is perplexing that women who have faced overt bias and discrimination refuse to call it bias and discrimination. Why do some women deny the fact that they have been discriminated against? I like Faye Crosby's (1984) explanation in an article titled "The Denial of Personal Discrimination." She argues:

It is as if women are completing a syllogism. The major premise states: "Women are discriminated against." The minor premise states: "I am a woman." But instead of the expected conclusion, "therefore I am discriminated against," women seem to say, "Phew, that was a close call." Such reasoning smacks of denial. (p. 372)

The women who deny that they have been discriminated against often see themselves as "exceptions." They argue that "I am not like other women; I am not a victim of sex discrimination, and my femaleness will not affect the work I do." As they dissociate themselves from their female identity, they remain self-oriented and tend not to identify with other women but rather with those who are the gatekeepers of the profession. They often do not provide support for girls or women and ignore issues of gender equity. Rather than offering a different voice, they perpetuate the status quo (Matthews, 1995).

There are also some uplifting stories among the 15 "wise and wonderful" storytellers; several report some positive experiences about being women in educational administration today and indicate that some things have changed for the better. There are also several who have championed women's ways of leading, which they say are different from those of many male administrators. Following are some of the positive and uplifting tales from the storytellers.

- Dolores and Marie tell of the support and encouragement from women's organizations such as the Women's Caucus of the American Association of School Administrators and Northwest Women in Education.
- Sarah, as the only female and Hispanic superintendent in the county, tells of the genuine acceptance and support from other male administrators and her emerging political awareness and effectiveness.
- Gail tells of mentoring and support from her male superintendent, who remains a friend and confidant.
- Elizabeth reflects the new concepts of leadership, which value those characteristics that have been stereotypically female: collaboration, facilitation, nurturing, support, and caring.

These changes are reflected in Chapter 9, "The Evolution of Issues Related to Leadership and Gender." Conceptually, this is the most important chapter in the book. Gupton and Slick focus on four shifts that have occurred in the past decades. Their identified shifts resonate with my experience also and are useful for individual women and advocacy groups for women to consider as we plan an agenda for the next century. They describe the following four shifts.

1. *A shift from women's lack of aspiration for administrative positions to their need for a better support system.* In 1975, I identified the "who, me?" woman. The "who, me?" woman was an administrator who had responded to an initial request that demanded responsibility and authority with "Who, *me*?" This woman questions her competence for leadership. I do not think there are many "who, me?" women in leadership today. I agree strongly with Gupton and Slick: We do not need to worry as much about motivating women to be administrators—we need to build support systems for them to compensate for the obstacles they still face just because they are women.

2. *A shift from women's lack of necessary qualifications and leadership ability to a greater concern about the quality of their preparation and recognition of their leadership talents.* There are two important issues here: preparation and leadership behaviors. Both issues have had attention over the past decades.

Preparation of school administrators is changing; it is moving from the paradigm of logical positivism and university elitism to a new respect for practitioners as theory builders and knowledge developers. It is an exciting time beginning to democratize educational administration.

Whereas, in the past, women were often given leadership training to compensate for their presumed lack of experience and knowledge, today we recognize that many women bring with them a way of leading that is different from the models of the past. The new model of leadership emphasizes collaboration, empowerment, and facilitation instead of controlling, directing, and bossing. Those new characteristics encompass many of the so-called female stereotypes. Whereas once the ideal administrator was decisive and rational, today the ideal administrator leads with the heart as well as the head (Sergiovanni, 1991). It is not coincidental that the model of leadership is changing as more women enter the arena of leadership. That is not to say that all women lead one way and all men lead another way; it is to say, however, that women and men have different cultural realities and experiences that lead to different ideas about leadership.

By including more diverse kinds of leaders, we have begun to conceptualize leadership differently from in the past.

3. *A shift from focusing solely on too few women acquiring positions in educational administration expanding to include on-the-job maintenance and retention issues.* Absolutely. The storytellers in this book describe on-the-job harassment and difficulty. Tallerico, Burstyn, and Poole's (1993) book on women superintendents who have left the field should give us cause to worry about retention. There are still Neanderthal thinkers—educators, school board members, and others who believe that women should not be in a leadership position. It may be lonely at the top; women at the top, however, face problems other than just loneliness. Stronger support systems need to be available to women administrators.

4. *The ultimate shift—from access to equity.* Gupton and Slick point out that old habits and time-honored gender roles are nebulous and stubbornly resistant to change. This has several implications for individuals and school organizations. I start from the premise that gender will be an operational variable for women in leadership. One cannot ignore it; gender and race make a difference whether one likes it or not. One can be aware of this fact and still make a difference—for oneself as well as for others.

What difference does it make that you are female? As individuals, women leaders must ascertain in what situations their femaleness matters. Sometimes, it will not matter at all; other times, it will matter very much. You need to know when it matters.

As a female leader, what difference will you make about gendered policy and practice in your organization? What stand will you take? When will you be the advocate for other girls or women in your organization? Some women leaders deny their female heritage by not addressing *any* issues about gender; they try to ignore it. One woman high school principal wanted to deny her femaleness. She said, "I bend over backwards *not* to give preferential treatment to women and girls in my school. I want to be an effective administrator, not an effective 'woman' administrator." She tried to be one of the boys and deny the fact that her femaleness made a difference. Other women leaders are activists; they effectively influence policy and practice in their schools. They know that they cannot take on all battles and that they cannot be seen as a single-issue administrator, but they are actively involved in creating greater gender equity.

Once women leaders were silent and invisible. In the past few decades, their silence and invisibility have been replaced with a new feminist consciousness and attention to their stories. This book adds to our knowledge and understanding of women leading.

Patricia Schmuck
Graduate School of Professional Studies
Lewis & Clark College

References

Crosby, F. (1984). The denial of personal discrimination. *American Behavioral Scientist, 27*, 371-386.

Kalvelage, J., Schmuck, P., & Smith, M. (1982). *Women getting together and getting ahead.* Newton, MA: Education Development Center.

Matthews, E. (1995). Women in educational administration: Views of equity. In D. M. Dunlap & P. A. Schmuck (Eds.), *Women leading in education*, pp. 247-273. Albany: SUNY Press.

Schmuck, P. (1975). *Sex differentials in school administration.* Arlington, VA: National Council of Administrative Women in Education.

Schmuck, P., & Schubert, J. (1995). Women principals' views on sex equity. In D. M. Dunlap & P. A. Schmuck (Eds.), *Women leading in education*, pp. 274-287. Albany: SUNY Press.

Sergiovanni, T. (1991). *The principalship: A reflective practice perspective.* New York: Allyn & Bacon.

Tallerico, M., Burstyn, J., & Poole, W. (1993). *Gender and politics at work: Why women exit the superintendency.* Fairfax, VA: National Policy Board for Educational Administration.

Preface

This book celebrates the professional and personal accomplishments of women in educational administration—many of whom are pioneers as women in top-level positions in the profession. The "voices" of these nationally representative women administrators often stir the reader's emotions as their stories unveil their trials and tribulations as well as their triumphant experiences in both pursuing and maintaining their professional goals for careers in administration, a field that continues to be male-oriented and male-dominated.

The knowledge base of organization and leadership theory is almost entirely derived from the white male perspective. Programs of preparation for teachers and administrators rely almost solely on literature exclusive of the female perspective. Experiences and insights of women, especially those in leadership positions, have yet to be explored widely and incorporated into the knowledge base. Despite *individual* similarities, with regard to *gender*, men and women clearly have differences in approaching tasks, dealing with people, and achieving career success. Our book should help to fill the void of readily available, existing information on women's insights and viewpoints regarding career achievement and leadership. There are many lessons to be learned from the wise and wonderful women whose voices rise from these pages. The women's accountings of their career success are woven into the text of our book as illustrative, poignant examples of what our research substantiates.

The research is irrefutable—despite their excellent qualifications and expressed aspirations, women in education continue to be under-represented in administration and to remain in those positions that are viewed more as the "behind the scenes" jobs. Ironically, although the numbers of women in executive-titled positions in the profession have increased recently, closer scrutiny of the positions they obtain reveals that their jobs frequently require longer hours, carry less power, and pay less than do similar positions held by their male counterparts.

Although an underrepresentation of women in educational administration persists, the reasons for this disparity have changed over the past 30 years. In part, the purpose of this book is to provide an up-to-date analysis of the evolution of issues underlying women's inequitable representation in executive positions in the profession. As former public school administrators, we initiated our research efforts because of our set of common experiences and interests regarding other women's experiences in educational administration. We were surprised to discover just how little information was available. We wanted to know why gender inequities persist after 25 years of affirmative action and in a nation supposedly sensitized to social consciousness. More important, we sought to discover why and how some women achieved, survived, and even thrived in top levels of organizational leadership. This book is a culmination of more than 4 years of collaborative research and shared reflection on this topic.

The chapter titles, represented by corresponding numbered lessons, are based on our analysis of the advice most often repeated to women aspiring to educational administration given by 151 randomly sampled women administrators included in our study. These women administrators—superintendents, assistant superintendents, and principals from all regions of the country—completed a 14-page questionnaire (Appendix A) on their experiences as female administrators in education; then, in a second phase of our research (Appendix B), 15 of the women were asked to tell in narrative form their personal stories of how they achieved their career success.

Each of the chapters includes information gleaned from the two-phase research described in the introduction. This book's content is based on our interpretation of the research data, which includes information from the questionnaires as well as the stories written by the women who participated in our research. At our request, the women told their stories in a conversational, informal way which oftentimes in print sounds awkward or may be structurally unusual. Thus, the "incorrections" in the stories should not be interpreted as the lack of scholarly ability.

Overview of Contents

Introduction—A review of related literature and a description of the research methodology and participants are presented in the introduction. Also included is our story of how we met and became involved in this research. Brief biographies of the 15 women whose stories we use extensively throughout the book conclude our introduction.

Chapter 1—Lesson 1: Be Prepared—focuses on the importance of preparation with the proper credentials as well as being prepared psychologically to overcome the barriers that women in particular encounter frequently in seeking a career in administration in the profession. It further explores the reality for women seeking administrative positions of having to go beyond being credentialed and skilled to being *outstanding*, more so than is typically expected of men in the profession.

Chapter 2—Lesson 2: Plan for *Your* Career—advises women to plan strategically for their careers as early as possible. This chapter is replete with caution regarding women's tendency early in their marriage to support their spouse's career goals to the neglect of their own. We discovered that all too frequently, women admitted stumbling into positions of authority or having to enter the workforce after a failed marriage, instead of using career savvy and strategy early in life. Because of the lack of career planning, the average age of female administrators is 10 to 15 years older than the average age of males entering administration.

Chapter 3—Lesson 3: Persevere—deals with the keys to sticking with it despite a host of barriers particularly associated with women seeking and achieving administrative careers. Not one of our research participants said that the pursuit of an administrative position would be easy; but they advised repeatedly, "Don't give up!" Their exemplary persistence will encourage and inspire readers.

Chapter 4—Lesson 4: Be Diligent and Professional—substantiates the perception that women in administrative positions are expected to work harder for less compensation and are usually scrutinized more critically than are male administrators. Professional behavior continues to be held to stricter standards for women in the executive suite. This chapter will provide guidance to aspiring female administrators regarding diligence, and it will address the importance of remaining patient, poised, and professional during the process.

Chapter 5—Lesson 5: Honor, Preserve, and Protect Your Integrity—emphasizes the virtue of having and maintaining utmost integrity and holding to one's principles despite political pressure that surely comes with ascending to and acquiring top-level positions. Ethics are critical to a woman's success in the profession, and according to our women, violation of one's ethics is never accepted where a woman is concerned. The double standard, say our women administrators, is still alive and responsible for the different rules for success for men and women. The ultimate messages these women convey are, "Know thyself, believe in thyself, and protect thyself!"

Chapter 6—Lesson 6: Reach Out to and Through Others—calls women into action by insisting on their developing political skill and prowess and in networking for support—both personally and professionally. Women have notoriously neglected these critically important career strategies. Our women's stories include a host of significant family members, professional organizations, and people who provided support and encouragement as the women pursued their careers.

Chapter 7—Lesson 7: Practice What You Seek: The Importance of Mentoring—extends the importance of women learning to develop stronger support systems by acquiring a career strategy well-known to men but frequently underused by women: the strategy of mentoring. The advice from our women administrators is direct and two-edged: "Have a mentor. And then, BE ONE!" Readers will learn about the characteristics of mentors and how they can favorably affect one's professional life.

Chapter 8—Lesson 8: Lead by Example—explores the leadership styles and strategies most employed by successful women leaders. Although the differences between the genders and their leadership preferences are acknowledged, the ultimate message is that today's complex organizations require creative, brave, transformational leadership talent potentially common to both genders but discovered only in the individual person. The leadership courage demonstrated by these women's stories is a source of inspiration to us all as they tell how they provide integrative, transformational leadership during a time of flux and uncertainty for schools and school systems across our nation.

Chapter 9—The Evolution of Issues Related to Leadership and Gender—briefly reviews historical perspectives on women in leadership positions in education and identifies important shifts that have taken place in relation to issues surrounding the underrepresentation of women in the field of educational administration. Many of the reasons for the gender inequity in administration in our profession have changed over the past 30 years; these changes are explored in this chapter.

Chapter 10—The Collective Voice: "Go for It!"—challenges women to seek leadership positions and believe in their capability to be top-level administrators. Repeatedly, the women caution women against perpetuating their own "glass ceiling" by not believing in themselves and their leadership potential. This final chapter is spiritual in nature because it relates the high level of enthusiasm and belief that our storytellers and respondents had in "going for the roses," "reaching for the stars," and believing that they could do it! Much like cheerleaders rooting for their team, our women's advice to other women was overwhelmingly "Go for it!" We felt this last chapter should be inspirational and optimistic. Certainly, this positive message accurately reflects the spirit of the stories and advice offered by our women participants. Our hope is that readers will gain insight into their own professional journeys through the stories shared by our women, and that, along with this insight, they will acquire additional knowledge that will assist them in their quest for leadership in education.

Throughout the book, we try to focus on the importance of seeking and nurturing outstanding leadership potential in the education profession regardless of gender. Indeed, organizations of all types are undergoing a redefinition of what is needed in today's leadership positions. The newer paradigms of leadership call for a gentler, more values-oriented integrative approach to leading. Although women leaders have been characterized as having a natural tendency by virtue of their gender to operate in this less autocratic manner, many men are equally capable of such a leadership style. "Circumstances surrounding leadership today," write Hill and Ragland (1995), "demand that we shed stereotypical images and seek leaders who are competent in fostering talents of others and skilled at unifying constituencies to address problems" (p. 6). The ultimate objective for the profession in seeking leadership should be to capitalize on the strengths of all people regardless of such irrelevant classifications as gender, race, or creed in order to harness and nurture the leadership needed so badly for today's complex school operation and for meeting the complex needs of today's children. To meet the challenges of leadership for the information age, leaders need to be creative, entrepreneurial, and willing to take and make risks in an increasingly rapid-changing world. "In all fields," contend Brooks and Regan in their 1995 publication on women's leadership, "men and women need to work together . . . to ensure that the perspectives of both genders are available for interpretation and instruction" (p. 111). The men and women capable of meeting these tough challenges will be a special breed of leaders that has learned to work with all people, to capitalize on the strengths that people as individuals bring to the collective effort of the organization, and to appreciate and even embrace differences among people and between the genders as being part of a healthy workforce. A workforce—indeed, a society—that is most productive and complete capitalizes on the strengths and perspectives of all people—complementing each other and bringing balance to the whole.

Acknowledgments

We are indebted to many people who should share the credit for making this book a reality. We begin at the beginning by recognizing our university's Center for Services and Resources for Women, which awarded us our initial research incentive funds of $250. We appreciate its support of women and research related to women's issues.

Throughout the 4 years of this study, our Vice President for Research and Planning, Dr. Karen Yarbrough, provided encouragement, advice, and exceptional financial backing, without which we could not have conducted our research. She is a constant source of strength and vision, not only for us but for our entire university and community.

Our good friends and colleagues, Genevieve Brown and Beverly Irby, with Sam Houston State University, helped us to believe in ourselves and the importance of our research. They and their affiliate group, The Texas Council of Women School Executives, gave us our first opportunity to publish part of our research results concerning the status of women in educational leadership. This first piece of writing, a chapter in a book edited by Brown and Irby and sponsored by the Council, was the impetus for further development of our study and ultimately provided the framework for this book (see Slick & Gupton, 1993). We are truly indebted to our Texas friends and the Council for sharing with us their expertise, their optimism, and, most of all, their genuine professional support and boundless spirit. We wish that all women had access to affiliations as positive, talented, and reaffirming as this Texas group.

We thank Stephanie Howard, a doctoral student and graduate assistant, who so capably assisted with correspondence, the bibliography, library material, and showed such genuine interest in our progress with the book. Our gratitude for behind-the-scenes support extends to Holly Rambin, Tammy Herrington, and Lauree Mills Mooney, whose able skills with the computer and editing helped us tremendously at different stages of the book. Their flexibility, conscientiousness, and cheerfulness were essential assets throughout the process of research and writing.

We wonder how authors can possibly do justice in an acknowledgments section to the countless, and many times subtle but deliberate, ways that supportive coworkers boost the development of a project as major as a book. A pat on the back, a thumbs-up sign, an encouraging word, sharing a newly discovered article related to our work, or inquiring about how the book was coming along meant so much to us and kept us going when we were experiencing setbacks and complications in the process. We both appreciate the genuine team spirit and support of our colleagues at the university.

We want to thank our secretaries, Tina Holmes and Sharon Hall, who were always there to help us meet deadlines; to protect us from interruptions when we needed some intensive, cooperative work time; to help us *find stuff*; and to believe in us and the importance of our work.

We are also grateful for the confidence expressed by our publisher, Corwin Press. Gracia Alkema, president of Corwin Press, and acquisitions editor Alice Foster have provided tremendous support and encouragement from the time of our proposal until the completion of the book. Corwin's editorial assistant, Nicole Fountain, has been a delightful, competent coworker as well. We feel fortunate to have contracted with these top-flight publishers; we could not have asked for more cooperative and positive people with whom to work.

We want to express our appreciation to Patricia Schmuck, Professor of Educational Leadership at Lewis and Clark College, for her willingness to write the foreword to our book and for her outstanding research and writing on issues related to women in educational leadership. Her work has helped to provide a much needed knowledge base about gender equity and women leaders' perspectives and to pave the way for better treatment of women in our profession.

Our families deserve very special acknowledgment. Eleanor Parker Lee, Sandra's mother, is the only surviving parent. Eleanor is a retired educator who was one of Sandra's teachers, as well as elementary principal, and was her first and remains her most significant role model as a female in educational administration. All of our parents, Weldon Ferdinand and Daisy Lea Guyon Appelt, Jacob Henry and Eleanor Parker Lee, were wonderfully supportive. They gave us life, nurtured us well, and provided through their own lives outstanding examples of leadership, courage, and strength that prepared us to be productive, well-adjusted, and confident women. Our upbringing continues to sustain us. The older we become, the more we appreciate the gifts of our parents, and the more we realize how very much like them we are.

Our children, Ginger Delane and Stacy Martha Gupton, Samantha Lea and Andrew Schiwetz-Slick, and Gloria's husband, Sam, were always behind us, willing to sacrifice their own share of our time and attention for "the book." From the inception of our research to the final production of our book, Sam has believed that our topic was significant and needed to be pursued through the research and writing we proposed. He has remained a strong supporter and advocate of our endeavors throughout the 5 years it took to reach our goal: the publication of this book. Our families' unwavering love and devotion to us and our career ambitions fueled our determination to put our very best effort into this book. Anything less would not merit the pride they take in us and our accomplishments. We are truly blessed with loving, supportive families who work together as a team and, as team members, are responsible for any successes we have as a part of our professional lives.

Finally, we thank all the women who contributed their time and reflective energy into responding to our lengthy questionnaire, which provided us with our initial insight into women leaders' perceptions of gender-related issues in the workplace in education. And to the 15 women who shared their personal, detailed stories of career successes and disappointments, we are greatly indebted to you. Without you and your personal courage and conviction to share with others so that their journeys toward leadership could be smoother and more comprehensible, this book would not have been possible. We wish you health, joy, Godspeed, and yes, even wealth, for you truly deserve such rewards! Thank you for giving all of us the courage to GO FOR IT!!

About the Authors

Sandra Lee Gupton, EdD, is an assistant professor with the Department of Educational Leadership and Research in the College of Education and Psychology at the University of Southern Mississippi, where she has been for the past 4 years. Before coming to the university, she worked for more than 20 years in public schools in Georgia and North Carolina as a teacher, principal, assistant superintendent, and superintendent of schools.

Since coming to USM, where she teaches courses in educational leadership, personnel administration, and curriculum development, she has published several articles related to her research interests in organizational leadership and the issues concerning underrepresentation of women in school administration.

Dr. Gupton attributes much of her career success to her number-one mentor, role model, and mother, Eleanor Parker Lee. Eleanor is a retired teacher and administrator respected and admired throughout Georgia for her contributions to the field. "Mother was providing leadership in education long before gender discrimination was even a familiar topic. I was truly blessed to have such a wonderful mother who taught me by daily example that women could do anything they wanted to do."

Gloria Appelt Slick, a native of Houston, Texas, completed her doctoral work at the University of Houston in 1979. Her professional career in public school education has included being a classroom teacher, curriculum supervisor, principal, assistant superintendent, and a federal program director. At the university level, Dr. Slick is an associate professor in the Department of Curriculum and Instruction as well as Director of the Office of Educational Field Experiences. For the past 5 years, she and Dr. Gupton have been engaged in intensive research concerning women in educational administration. In addition to this research interest, Dr. Slick has published four books with Corwin Press dealing with field experiences in teacher preparation programs. She brings a comfortable blend of public school and higher education professional experiences to this current writing. Dr. Slick is empathetic to women's concerns regarding educational administration because, for the past 30 years, she too has experienced the issues related to women in the profession.

Introduction

Our Story

We met for the first time late in the Fall 1991 semester at the University of Southern Mississippi. It was Sandra's first year and Gloria's second year at this institution. Our dean had indicated to Sandra that she might like to meet Gloria sometime since our professional careers had been somewhat similar. At the time we met, Sandra was a first-year Assistant Professor in the Department of Educational Research and Leadership. Gloria was in her second year as Director, Office of Educational Field Experiences, and Assistant Professor in the Department of Curriculum and Instruction. We had both been public school classroom teachers for several years, building principals, and assistant superintendents. Sandra was also an acting superintendent. Gloria had also been a federal program director and an education specialist at a regional service center. Most of Sandra's public school experience had been in North Carolina, and Gloria's was in Texas. Although we were separated by many miles and in different regions of the country, our professional experiences had been very similar.

The first time we met, it was due to a flyer sent around by a campus women's group sponsoring research related to women. The group offered a small research stipend to interested faculty who wished to pursue research related to topics concerning women.

Almost simultaneously, we thought of each other and the comment our dean had made about our needing to get together. Our thoughts about the kind of research we would like to do were incredibly similar. We wanted to know what other women's experiences in their quest for, ascent to, and acquisition of leadership positions in the profession had been. We were awarded a $250 research stipend and the rest is history. Today, 5 years later, we find ourselves more closely aligned both personally and professionally. Our spirit of camaraderie has only grown more deeply, and our commitment to share with and learn from other women like ourselves burns strong. This book is about that commitment and the belief that we share that all administrators, both female and male, can benefit from the experiences and struggles, as well as successes, that the women we write about in our book reveal through their responses to the questionnaire and in their stories.

Before designing our own research process and the instruments we used to obtain information about women in educational leadership, we surveyed the literature relevant to our research. We were surprised to discover that very little research had been done concerning women in educational leadership for the past decade. We then began to realize that it was not just our personal need and desire to research the current status of women in educational leadership, but that there definitely was an overall professional need to determine the status of women in leadership in the education profession.

Background: Related Literature and Selected Research Results

The underrepresentation of women in educational administration is more than an issue of gender inequity; oppressive behaviors and practices within the profession are stifling and will ultimately serve no one well. "Gross inequities played out in one part of the educational system," Jackie Blount (1993) admonishes in her dissertation on the topic, "will inevitably be perpetuated in others" (p. 29). Because of the far-reaching implications of this issue, we chose to investigate the topic further in order to learn more about the experiences and perceptions of today's women administrators in education. We sought to add more current quantitative and qualitative data to the research base and literature that exists about women executives and their beliefs, background, and experiences, as well as their advice to other women and men in the profession. Since 1980, the number of women in superintendents' positions alone has increased from less than 1% to more than 6% nationally (and some sources put this figure as high as 11%). Although this appears to be a healthy growth on the surface, it is important to take a closer look at the quality of the positions being procured. Many times, the positions being filled by women are those that have a minimal power base because they are in smaller, more rural school districts. Even so, this new breed of women executives in education should be able to provide a wealth of information about their experiences that could be useful to other women pursuing administrative careers. These women's experiences should also benefit practicing administrators in their work to ensure a more bias-free workplace through improved personnel practices, policy, and the overall working relationships between the genders.

As a result of our own experiences in public school education, we knew that gender issues were a factor in the workplace. Our common experiences and the desire to determine the status of women currently in the workplace motivated us to proceed with the two phases of research described in the preface.

Major themes or issues emerged as we reviewed the literature in preparation for the research we wanted to conduct concerning women's underrepresentation in educational administration. A description of what we discovered pertaining to each of the themes follows.

Women's Lack of Aspiration for Administrative Positions

An increasing number of women hold certification and degrees to qualify them for administrative positions (women received 11% of the doctoral degrees in educational administration in 1971, 20% in 1980, 39% in 1982, and 49% in 1991). Recent numbers reported by Quality Education Data, Inc. (1992) indicate that approximately 10% of school superintendents, 22% of assistant superintendents, and 9% of high school principals in the United States are women. These three positions are considered the power positions in public school education. Although these figures look promising, little change has been documented in the predominant cultural and social patterns within organizations that have historically posited women in subordinate instructional roles and men in the power roles of administration:

"two separate, mutually dependent professions" (Ortiz & Marshall, 1988, p. 123). The implication is that the "good old boy" system continues to thrive. This was corroborated by our respondents in the 14-page questionnaire when an overwhelming majority (92%) either strongly agreed or agreed that the "good old boy" system is alive and well in educational administration. A closer look at specifics such as district size, population demographics, and operating budget indicates that the increase of women superintendents has occurred "primarily in very small districts or involves minority women in urban districts that enroll predominantly minority students" (Ortiz & Marshall, 1988, p. 127). So, even though women are achieving administrative status, it is not occurring frequently in larger districts, which both regionally and nationally wield the greatest deal of influence in the profession.

Another aspect affecting women's aspirations to leadership positions frequently is a lack of clear professional goals. Studies (e.g., Bonuso & Shakeshaft, 1983; Thomas, 1986; Weber, Feldman, & Poling, 1981) often show a strong correlation between women's lack of career advancement and their lower career goals. In our own research, our respondents reported more frequently than we expected that they had not carefully planned their ascent to the top. It seems that often opportunities had simply emerged and they pursued their options in an unplanned manner. Sometimes, a mentor or a boss suggested that they apply for a position. Other times, their acquisition of a position was by default, tenure in the district, and/or because they had completed an advanced degree and were available. Newman (1978) suggests that women frequently have had to compromise their career aspirations because of inner conflict created by family responsibilities and role identification. Conversely, women who have achieved executive positions in education frequently demonstrate a strong desire to succeed and view themselves as leaders despite the dominant stereotype in this society of white male leadership (Benton, 1980; Pavan, 1989; Swiderski, 1988). In a recent study, Gallese (1991) interviewed 24 highly ranked female executives and reported that

> those women who broke into the senior ranks did so because male bosses didn't allow common misconceptions about women's capacity for power to cloud their judgment, and because the women were themselves comfortable with pursuing power. The women who failed, by contrast . . . didn't scramble as aggressively for power. (p. 18)

Unfortunately, our research revealed that many women aspire to less than the top-level administrative positions in the profession. Many still see themselves in a supportive role even in administration. The majority of our 151 respondents were in assistant superintendent positions rather than in the "chief" positions of superintendent or high school principal. Forty-nine percent of our respondents were assistant superintendents, 29% were superintendents, and 21% were high school principals. The majority of our assistant superintendents were in the area of curriculum and instruction, an area traditionally staffed by women. In summary, although more women are clearly aspiring to administrative positions, the positions they acquire are less than the most powerful in the profession.

Cultural Stereotypes Regarding Gender, Roles, and Leadership

A growing body of research attests to the outstanding leadership potential of women in all administrative positions (McGrath, 1992). A study recently released by Russell Reynolds Associates found that significantly more female executives display leadership potential than do their male counterparts (Gallese, 1991). Several studies on principals' leadership qualities have found women to be even more effective than men as instructional leaders (Andrews & Basom, 1990; Tibbetts, 1980). Such findings run counter to the myth that leadership ability belongs primarily to the male gender.

Attitudinal studies consistently show a bias against women compared with men for school administrative positions. This bias is found among teachers, school board members, and superintendents (Ortiz & Marshall, 1988). Furthermore, the literature is replete with claims of sex role stereotyping as the major barrier to women seeking entry into or advancement in educational administration. As Kathleen Lynch (1990) reports, "In spite of more than thirty years of data to the contrary, the myth remains that the ideal manager conforms to a masculine stereotype" (p. 2). No longer is education or certification seen as the primary obstacle; instead, the main impediment to women's career advancement seems to be the unstated but understood requirements that aspiring candidates must look and act like those already in power. This attitude is pervasive and seems typical of both those in power and others, including, ironically, women themselves within the profession (Garland, 1991; Gotwalt & Towns,

1986; Ortiz & Marshall, 1988). When we queried our respondents in the questionnaire about their perceptions regarding the lack of equitable representation of women in educational administration, the number-one reason identified was cultural stereotyping of "appropriate" roles for men and women. Many of the women who shared their personal stories with us also related experiences that verified the existence of continued sex role stereotyping as a major impediment to women aspiring to administration. It is almost as if Marie, one of our study's respondents, had challenged sacred ground by aspiring to be an administrator. She relates:

> I applied for several administrative positions in my home district without receiving any. I was told that to be an administrator, one must first "pay your dues." Paying dues meant working one's way up through coaching, to vice principal, to principal; and I had never been a coach. The district apparently feared that I would file a discrimination suit.

Both our own research and our review of related literature bear out the perceptions and experiences reported to us by our women administrative respondents. In general, leadership positions in education are typically held by males, and the prevailing social perspective continues to be that men belong in those leadership positions. Even though there are more and more women achieving leadership positions in the profession, the numbers are still very low compared with the number of men in those positions. Another respondent, Elizabeth, provides another example of attitudes that frequently persist in our profession relative to women in leadership positions:

> Since I had a master's degree by this time in English, I decided to apply for the position of Secondary English Supervisor when it became available. All of the supervisors' positions until that time had been held by men. I was the first woman to apply. When I got the job, the curriculum director told me that I had gotten the job because I was female, and they were afraid the Office of Civil Rights would become involved if they didn't have at least one woman among the five or six supervisors.

So, under the possible threat of legal action being taken against them, this district hired a woman for a central office job. It is sad to think that it takes this kind of coercion in today's world for women or anyone to be given an equal opportunity to obtain a job. What really is important is that both men and women are given equal opportunities to have access to and be supported in positions of leadership in the profession, and that their procurement of any one of those positions is based upon their individual abilities and not on sex role stereotypes.

As women have grappled for opportunities to become administrators in the profession, they have had to wrestle with the type of persona they must project in the executive office. Many women have attempted to cloak themselves with male administrative styles. Men often use "transactional" leadership, doling out rewards for good work and punishment for bad (Billard, 1992). Traditionally, men's style of leadership has tended to be more authoritarian and direct. Giving orders, directing, and overseeing all transactions, as well as being the final word in all decisions regarding operational procedures, are the typical characteristics of men's leadership style. The authoritarian style of leadership has prevailed for so long in the profession that any departure from such has often been viewed as weak and ineffective. According to many sources, however, women do have their own style of leadership that tends to be more transformational than authoritarian. Transformational leaders engage others in decision making; they share power and information, thereby providing a type of leadership that involves all concerned and affected by professional decisions.

This participatory, integrative style of leadership motivates members of the organization by transforming their self-interest into the goals of the organization (Billard, 1992). This prompted our interest in our respondents' perceptions of their own leadership style. Included in the questionnaire was a list of leadership characteristics. The respondents were asked to indicate how they thought of themselves with regard to certain leadership characteristics. When comparing themselves with their male counterparts, the respondents viewed themselves as *more* verbally oriented, *more* concerned about personal relationships, and *more* cooperative than males in similar positions. Interestingly, they saw themselves as basically the *same* as their male counterparts with regard to being aggressive, competitive, spatially oriented, career oriented, family oriented, and androgynous. Respondents indicated that they were *less* like men in one characteristic: being motivated by power. The three characteristics that the women perceived themselves as possessing *more* than men are related to the transformational leadership style.

Terrence Deal contends that the movement toward participatory management involves transforming the basic character of schools (Lunenburg & Ornstein, 1991). He views schools as a culture and believes that the structures within the system or culture of public schools cannot be reformed, but must be transformed. Steven Berglas thinks the female style of leadership is better positioned for hard times: "In an era when the need to motivate is so important, women will do better because they are nurturers and value driven" (Billard, 1992, p. 70). It is interesting to note that our women respondents see themselves as equally strong as leaders in some areas typically attributed to male leadership style: aggression and competition. Although, as Berglas says, women are typically perceived to be nurturers, our women perceive themselves to be capable leaders, which includes characteristics of aggression as well as a competitive spirit. Almost to a person, however, they do fit the value-driven characteristic to which Berglas refers. In fact, many of the study's women indicated that they aspired to leadership positions because they wanted to make a positive difference for children.

Inadequate Training and Educational Opportunity

Although an increasing number of women hold certification and degrees to qualify them for administrative positions, inadequate training and educational opportunity are frequently among the top few explanations cited in the literature for women's underrepresentation in executive positions in education (Lambert, 1989; Rogers & Davis, 1991; Short et al., 1989; Whitecraft & Williams, 1990). As previously noted, however, there has been a consistent pattern of increase in numbers of women seeking the doctorate in educational administration—11% in 1972, 20% in 1980, and 39% in 1982 (Ortiz & Marshall, 1988). With this increase, concern is being shifted to how adequate and appropriate the education programs and training are. Even so, Marie, one of our 15 women, related experiencing the following when she began her quest for administrative credentials:

I learned that some courses in school administration were being taught in our part of the state. I signed up for one only to learn that it was taught during the day on school days when teachers were working with children. It was then that I learned about the "old boy network"—attractive and promising young male administrators were invited by their superiors to become administrators. The members of school administration classes were already in administrative positions while taking courses to become qualified for the job. The fact that I was an uninvited participant in one of their courses made me a very fractious individual in the eyes of administrators in my district as well as the surrounding districts.

Fifty-five percent of our respondents to the questionnaire ranked inadequate training and educational opportunity in the top three reasons for women's underrepresentation in educational administration.

Shakeshaft (1986a) contends that females' intellectual growth is not particularly nurtured by schools. She suggests that the treatment of females in class as well as in content of books and materials used in schools contributes to women's feelings of inferiority and lowered aspirations. Similar to the concern for the restructuring of knowledge and changes in curriculum to incorporate feminine perspectives is what Ken Kempner (1989) refers to as the *culture of education administration,* a culture that is dominated by male orientations. "It is apparent," writes Kempner, "that women, minorities, and others who do not share the physical, social and cultural attributes of those who currently predominate in educational administration do not find easy access to the castle [of administration]" (p. 120). University programs in education perpetuate the exclusion of administrative females to top-ranking positions with curricula based primarily on models of authoritative style leadership (Glazer, 1990). According to Kempner (1989),

Individuals not possessing domineering characteristics are considered incapable of the rigors required of administrators who prescribe to an authoritarian conception of leadership. Those individuals who do not possess these characteristics, notably women and minorities, face extraordinary difficulty in entering and surviving in educational administration. (p. 119)

In essence, what Kempner, Shakeshaft, Choldin, Ortiz, and others in the field advocate is more serious, systematic attention to restructuring scholarship and training in educational administration. These scholars concur that training programs should include the values, needs, priorities, and leadership perspectives of women that have not been dealt with by the dominant organizational theorists to date. Administrative training and administrators' roles must be evaluated and updated to ensure the best possible training for educational leaders of both genders (Ginn, 1989; Shakeshaft & Nowell, 1984; Styer, 1989). If the profession is going to benefit from the talents of both men and women, a new attitude regarding who can lead must emerge and be viewed as viable and possible. Such an attitude begins in the institutions of higher education where the training of future administrators occurs.

Insufficient Support Systems for and Among Women

The lack of networking, the scarcity of positive role models, and inadequate sponsorships and mentoring among women are often cited as major barriers to women's career advancement in educational administration, as well as executive positions across all professions (Benton, 1980; Coursen, 1989; Green, 1982; Johnson, 1991; Mellow, 1988; Rist, 1991; Swiderski, 1988; York et al., 1988). In a recent C-SPAN program, Women of Washington—Forum on Women and Politics, sponsored by *Newsweek,* one of the panelists indicated that one of the most significant reasons women did not enter the political arena was due to the lack of a network. Men have the usual "good old boy" network to assist them, but women traditionally have had very little support in the political or professional arenas. In our own study, responses to the questionnaire identified *insufficient role-modeling, networking, and mentoring among women* as the second most prevalent reason women were underrepresented in positions of leadership in the profession. In their answers to the questionnaire, our respondents indicated the importance of having both personal and professional advocates as they proceeded toward their leadership goals. Many related that the support of family members made it possible for them to achieve their goals. Others spoke of professional mentors, some of whom were men, who encouraged them in their leadership pursuits. When asked if they were a part of a "strong network of supportive women in the profession," 41% of our respondents indicated that they were, and another 40% indicated interest in being a part of a strong network. Curiously, however, just under 17% responded that they did not see a need for a strong supportive network of women. Of course, it is difficult to see a need for one when there are so few women available in top administrative positions to be mentors. It is encouraging that more than 80% of respondents to the questionnaire indicated that they had been a mentor to someone in the profession.

Description of the Study

We conducted two phases of research that initially surveyed 300 randomly selected, top-level female administrators in public school education. The women surveyed hold positions as superintendents, assistant superintendents, and high school principals, which are perceived to be the power positions in public school. One hundred fifty-one women (51%) responded to the first phase of our research, which consisted of a 14-page questionnaire. The questionnaire was designed by us, and it solicited personal data, beliefs, and perceptions of women in the workplace from our respondents. The questionnaire was devoted entirely to soliciting information about these women administrators' experiences with and perceptions about their ascent to the top. The 14-page questionnaire was mailed to the potential respondents in the fall of 1992. Responses were returned in the late fall and early spring of 1993. We made the decision to include the breadth of topics related to the study of women in educational leadership even though it meant that the instrument would be lengthier than is typically recommended for mail questionnaires. Each section of the questionnaire dealt with issues found in the related literature to be relevant to women achieving top-level positions in the profession. The sections of the questionnaire included (a) beliefs about women's issues in the workplace; (b) career paths—career motives and beliefs, professional career experiences, career-related barriers, and career assessment; (c) significant life influences affecting career—positive role models, negative role models, mentors, and mentoring behavior; (d) leadership characteristics; (e) demographics; and (f) best advice for women aspiring to be administrators. Compensation for the length of the instrument was believed to be reflected in the highly appropriate sample of respondents and the importance of the topic to the women sampled. The final format of the questionnaire included a variety of response options that were selected to match the nature of the data requested. The thoroughness of the responses provided by the participants offered evidence that they believed both the questionnaire and their responses were very important. The responses were reflective and poignant in nature. Many of our respondents thanked us for the opportunity to reflect upon their careers and the processes involved in achieving their top-level positions in the profession. The questionnaire allowed for both concise, quantitative responses as well as short answer/essay responses that were more qualitative in nature. Therefore, the respondents were able to essentially experience both a professional and personal catharsis through the process of responding to the questionnaire. Consequently, the data were rich with information that sometimes substantiated and sometimes shattered conventional ideas related to women's experiences in the workplace.

Subsequent to the initial 14-page questionnaire, we solicited a select group of women from the initial group of respondents to participate in the second phase of our research. The 25 women we contacted had indicated on the original questionnaire that they would be interested in participating in more in-depth research on our topic of women in educational administration. We sent these 25 women letters inviting them to tell their stories of their ascent to the top. Of the 25 women invited, 15 took the time and energy to relate their personal stories. Along with a letter of invitation to participate in this second phase, we sent a two-page set of demographic questions and narrative prompts to assist the participants in telling their stories. We purposely wanted our participants to focus freely on their individual experiences and to present information and events that they felt were important to share. Therefore, we had no specific required format or process for them to use in sharing their stories. Some of our respondents chose to write their stories in their own handwriting, much like a letter being written to friends; others used word processing; and still others audiotaped their stories. To be sure, all of the stories were revealing, interesting, informative, and heartwarming. We greatly appreciate these women and the courage they exhibited in sharing their stories so that others might benefit from their experiences. The stories of these 15 women serve to reinforce and give vivid examples of the more objective data gleaned from the original questionnaire. Also included in each chapter are comments made by respondents who participated in the first phase of our research, the 14-page questionnaire.

In a comparative analysis of the data compiled by comparing the three top-level administrative positions of our women respondents, we discovered that 73% of the women superintendents were employed in rural school districts, 5% in urban school districts, and 21% in suburban school districts. Forty-three percent of the women holding assistant superintendent positions were located in suburban school districts, 32% were in urban school districts, and 24% were in rural school districts. Assistant superintendents were more evenly distributed across all types of districts than either superintendents or high school principals. Women high school principals were most prevalent in rural school districts (42%). The next largest representation of women high school principals was in suburban school districts (38%). Only 19% of women high school principals were located in urban school districts. It is evident from this analysis that when it comes to the top position (superintendent) in school districts, women are overwhelmingly occupying rural school district positions, the positions that wield less political power and have less financial weight in the overall scheme of the profession. These positions do not command the high-level salaries of larger school districts, and the stories of some of our contributors further verify this trend.

Because our book is based on the literature and our own extensive research, which includes the personal stories of women in educational administration positions in the profession, we feel that we are offering readers a unique opportunity to receive information regarding the most contemporary and thorough research in the field. In both phases of our research, there emerged some important lessons related to the success of these women. These lessons of advice and/or experiential knowledge are the focus of this book. The personal experiences of our 15 women lend a vivid dimension to each chapter.

Whenever possible, we chose a single story that best represented a lesson to present in each chapter. Often, however, more than one of our stories had a portion related to a lesson; in that case, we share pieces of several stories to best provide readers with a variety of points of view related to that theme or lesson. Many times, the difference between achieving a dream and continuing only to dream is the belief that a dream can come true. The stories presented throughout the book are inspirational and will give courage to those women who believe they have something special to offer children and the profession that exists for those children. The reader will gain insight into her or his own professional journey to the top that will be both beneficial and encouraging. Along with this insight, individuals will acquire some knowledge and skills that will assist them in their quest for leadership in the profession.

Study Participants

As mentioned earlier, this research project and book grew out of our relationship and shared common experiences as women in educational leadership positions. We discovered that our common paths had exposed us to similar situations as women, and we were wondering if other women had experienced the same or similar circumstances. We now feel a strong bond with all our respondents and storytellers who have so openly and courageously shared their lives and experiences with us. We feel privileged to know them in a very personal way, even though we have never met them. We experienced a kindred spirit with our newfound friends and sensed a profound need in these women to have the opportunity to share their feelings and experiences with others who have walked similar paths. So that you, the reader, can get to know us and these wonderful women better, we are going to provide you with some more personal information about each one; while you are reading about their experiences, you will be able to relate better to their stories. Even though our storytellers agreed to allow their names to be used in our book, we felt that pseudonyms were more appropriate. These people are too special to us for us to risk jeopardizing their personal and/or professional lives in any way. You may ask why relating a true story might be potentially harmful to an individual? Sadly, our caution with regard to these women's anonymity is, in part, a reflection of the status of women in the profession. Yes, strides have been made that are providing more opportunities for women in our profession, but more needs to happen both in the profession and in society before a true perception of the outstanding contributions women can make to the profession will be truly appreciated and understood.

From the national survey of 300 randomly selected female executives in education, the 51% who responded to the questionnaire represented various ethnic groups. The racial composition consisted mainly of Caucasian women (87%). However, there was some representation from other ethnic groups, including African American (6%), Hispanic

(4.7%), and Native American (2%). With the minority populations emerging toward a majority, it would appear that a more equitable representation of women among the various ethnic groups should be forthcoming.

Seventy-four percent of the respondents indicated that they had married only once, and of those, 60.9% were still in those marriages. Twelve percent were currently divorced, and 10% were single and had never been married. Twenty-three percent of the respondents indicated that they had been married twice, and another group (28.5%) indicated that they had been divorced at least once. The average age of our respondents representing the top three administrative levels in public schools was 49 years. Ninety-five percent of them reported having good health. In regard to the possible health concerns mentioned in the questionnaire, 14.6% reported stress as being an issue. The majority of the women (68.2%) indicated that they did not have any health concerns. Our questionnaire did indicate that our respondents are health conscious. Seventy-one percent indicated that they were practicing good nutrition, 61.7% said that they exercised regularly, 55.5% indicated that they engaged in recreational activities, and 58.6% reported that they took time to relax.

Many of our respondents had families who were very supportive as the women endeavored to reach their professional goals. There was an average number of two children in their families, but as many as six and seven for a few. Even though our respondents indicated that family support was critical and that they sometimes felt that their families might have suffered from the extensive time and effort the women had to give to accomplish their goals, a large majority of the women (more than 75%) indicated that they would pursue their career goals if they had to do it all over again. They also soundly dispelled the notion that a woman in a leadership position had to sacrifice her femininity to achieve a top-level position. Ninety percent of our respondents either disagreed or strongly disagreed with the survey's statement *my femininity has been diminished as a result of my career as an executive.*

Our respondents are active professionally in many organizations. Fifty-six percent of them hold membership in the Association of Supervision and Curriculum Development. Another 47% of them are members in the American Association of School Administrators.

Conclusion

The reader will enjoy getting to know our respondents and experiencing vicariously their journey to the top. There will be a relationship of immediate rapport as women aspiring to become administrators, as well as those who are already in those positions, read the personal stories of women like themselves who have struggled to achieve their professional goals. The book is intended to provide women who desire to be in, or already are in, leadership positions with insight into their situations, as well as show them how to go about achieving their professional goals. Women will find themselves inspired and encouraged by the stories and information presented in this book to continue their quest to be leaders in the profession. This, we hope, is the beginning of a new era of leadership where the talents of women and men are recognized equitably so that our children will benefit from the best of both genders.

We now present our friends and colleagues.

Marie: Growing up in a large farming family, Marie learned that to make it to the top, one had to work hard. As one of only four women superintendents in her state, she has, in fact, succeeded at reaching the top. Because both of Marie's parents were in postsecondary education before starting their family, it was a natural career choice for her.

Marie graduated with honors in 1954 from one of her home state universities and received her master's degree in 1976. After her three children were grown, she moved to another city and began working in special education, then went on to become an elementary principal in her home state. Marie also worked with her state's department of education before taking her present job as superintendent of a small school district.

Marie's Advice: Be strong, establish your own ethics and morals, and act according to them. Be willing to take risks in order to do what's right.

Nell: As a wife and mother of two, Nell credits her husband and family for giving her strength. She credits her mother, who was also an administrator, for teaching her the kind of perseverance that led to her success in administration. Nell grew up in a small town in the South, where she remains.

Nell received her bachelor's degree in 1967, a master's in education in 1974, and a doctorate in 1979. She served as a teacher in and out of her home state for 10 years, going on to serve as administrative assistant for a county school district for 12 years. Nell is currently working as assistant superintendent of a small school district in her home state.

Nell's Advice: Stay focused on your goal and never give up. Remember that education is a team effort, everyone working together for the students.

Elizabeth: Elizabeth, an assistant superintendent in her home state, began her career as a seventh-grade teacher. Both her mother and father were teachers who gave her much support. Elizabeth also received much support from her mentors—teachers and educational employers—and has gained much motivation from books.

Elizabeth holds a bachelor's, master's, and doctorate in education as well as many educational certificates. She is married with one son. In addition to teaching Grades 7 through 12, she has also worked as an executive director of special programs, an educational consultant, a graduate instructor, a supervisor of secondary English and reading, and a coordinator of secondary gifted programs.

Elizabeth's Advice: Interact with others in your field. You can learn so much by sharing experiences and ideas. Don't be afraid to take risks. Read as much as you can and always strive to learn more.

Freda: Freda had supportive parents who encouraged her to become a math teacher. She became very involved with children who needed special care, role modeling, and nurturing. Out of this concern for children from dysfunctional, lower socioeconomic situations, Freda decided to pursue a career in educational administration. A strong mentoring relationship that still exists today helped her to strive toward her educational goals.

After receiving her doctorate, Freda was employed by a state department of education. Later, she became an assistant superintendent for instruction. She is currently a freelance educational consultant.

Freda married toward the end of her doctoral program. She had three young children to care for when her marriage ended. Her children are now grown.

Freda's Advice: Keep trying—but mostly do whatever you do well. Don't be afraid to do more and to take on more responsibility.

Brenda: Originally from the Northeast, Brenda recently served as superintendent in a very large K-12 school district with a fiscal management in the millions. The district consisted of a number of consolidated districts, thereby making Brenda responsible to several boards.

Brenda is married and has two grown children. She received her master's in school administration at a northern university in 1976 and received her doctorate in education in 1980. Within a year after receiving her degree, she became an administrator as a junior high principal.

Brenda is no longer in the above-mentioned superintendent position. She resigned, citing political undermining as her principle reason. The physical and emotional strain, she indicated, were not worth putting up with in order to remain.

Brenda's Advice: Have a strong support system in place while you are in a job. Network heavily with other women superintendents. Don't go it alone any more than you'd walk through Central Park at night!

Sarah: Sarah grew up in a small farming community during World War II, during a time when women were viewed only as housewives and mothers. After her brothers were drafted, leaving only herself to do the farming chores, Sarah began to gain feelings of liberation, equality, and confidence about establishing a career. Since teaching seemed to be a somewhat lucrative woman's career, Sarah finished high school and began college to study education. Because of a shortage of teachers in her state at that time, Sarah was granted a temporary teaching certificate while still attending college and began teaching elementary school.

After receiving her bachelor's degree in 1957, Sarah became pregnant and soon left her teaching position. Sarah went on to raise six children before returning to her career in 1965. She continued teaching until 1973, when she received her master's degree. Soon after, she took a job as elementary principal and went on to become the first female in her state to be appointed district superintendent. Sarah is currently serving as superintendent of a small rural district in her home state.

Sarah's Advice: Strive until you can reach no further in your career, but never neglect yourself or your family along the way.

Emily: Beginning her career as a high school teacher, Emily found education to be a challenging and fulfilling job. Her love for children led her to return to graduate school to gain elementary teaching credentials to add to her secondary experience. She began working with troubled youths and special education students, then went on to accept a high school principalship in a small logging town.

Being female and married and having two young children, Emily was not well received in her traditionally male position. Because of continued negativity, she left that position after 2 years and currently serves as assistant superintendent in a district with an enrollment of about 3,000.

Emily received her bachelor's degree in 1964 and went on to receive a master's in education in 1975. She is currently working toward her Ph.D.

Emily's Advice: Be a "go-getter." Work toward what you want and be determined to get it. Maintain your personal ethics and integrity. Work hard, but always take time for yourself and your family. The job is not worth being a second-rate person, mother, and wife.

Diane: After graduating high school and receiving a 2-year degree in liberal arts, Diane married and later had her first child. She commuted 120 miles in order to continue college and received her bachelor's degree in 1976. She taught high school French and history while working toward her master's degree, then served as principal of an elementary school. Her husband is also in education.

Diane went on to receive her doctorate in education in 1989 and has been serving in her current position as superintendent since 1991. Diane says her three children (now grown) learned by example of both her and her husband the importance of education and hard work.

Diane's Advice: Don't view your being turned down for a job as something negative about yourself. People will expect more from you as a female leader. You must earn respect by deed.

Harriet: Harriet came to the United States as a sixth grader, unable to speak English until she reached high school. Even though her language deficiency resulted in low SAT scores, she enrolled in a local university, graduated, and began teaching Spanish and U.S. history while working toward a counseling degree. After 7 years of teaching, Harriet became assistant principal of a local high school. She developed programs for limited-English students to help them educationally as well as peer clubs to help them socially. Harriet worked hard to see that limited-English students would not suffer from the lonely, helpless feelings that she had experienced as a student.

Today, Harriet works as a district administrator in her state's largest school system, in the same district where she struggled as a student. She is married and has two teenage children.

Harriet's Advice: Work hard, not only for yourself, but also for your students. It is one's duty to target the needs of all children, minority or otherwise.

Gail: Gail, a superintendent in a small northern school district, grew up with the typical notion that women were limited in their career choices. She spent her first year of college studying to become a nun, but left the postulancy to attend a public college and study music education. She taught K-12 music and taught one year of seventh-grade English. She obtained her master's, and then received her doctorate in 1984. She took a job as an assistant principal in her state and went on to serve two different high school principalships, then held a position of director of curriculum and instruction. Because of budget cutbacks, she was laid off from this position and began looking for a superintendency. She served as superintendent of a 800-student district before moving to her present position.

Gail is a single, working mother with three adopted daughters. She currently serves as a superintendent for a 2,200-student district in her home state.

Gail's Advice: Get all the education and experience you can and continue to work your way up the ladder until you get where you want to be.

Jane: With more than 65 years in education, Jane's first teaching experience was in a one-room rural school, which meant teaching all grades and subjects, carrying water, and building fires. After teaching for several years, Jane finally received her degree in 1955 and her master's in 1958. She continued her career as a high school teacher. Not only did she serve in her teaching capacity, but she also became involved with the students as a class sponsor, attending sporting events, raising money, directing school plays, and coordinating proms.

Today, Jane is a county superintendent, a position that she has held for more than 19 years.

Jane's Advice: If you want a position in administration, Go For It! Never give up until you reach your goal. Women can do as much and just as well as men!

Delores: An assistant superintendent from the Northwest, Delores is married and holds a bachelor's, master's, and doctorate degree in education. Delores credits her parents for instilling her with a high value of education. As a ninth-grader, she decided to follow the career of teaching and was always supported by her family. Even after her leg was nearly amputated in an accident, she was determined to achieve her goal and returned to college soon after her hospital stay. Delores walked with crutches for 3 months as she continued her education.

Within a few months of receiving her degree, Delores landed her first teaching job near her home town. She went on to receive her doctorate and was the first woman (and the only one since) to hold office as president of her state's association of school administrators.

Delores's Advice: Remember the importance of family and friends. They are an invaluable source of strength. Try to be a source of strength to others and offer your help and advice to women like yourself who are beginning their career in education. Always remain dedicated to yourself, your goals, and your cause.

Catherine: Catherine serves as a deputy superintendent in her state. She is married and has one teenage son. Although she has much experience and many talents in her field, Catherine never received a college degree. She blames her lack of formal education for hindering her climb up the professional ladder. Many times, she was discriminated against for her lack of a degree, being passed up for positions or being paid less than a college graduate for the same skills and duties.

Catherine learned many of her skills from a deputy superintendent who mentored her during the beginning years of her career. Through him, she also gained the personal qualities and ethics that she so strongly maintains today. Even with the many obstacles she faced, Catherine has succeeded in her career and has managed to maintain her integrity along the way.

Catherine's Advice: Always go after your dreams—never sacrifice your own dreams for someone else's success. Don't let people mistreat you if you haven't done anything wrong. If you believe in yourself—don't hold back!

Denise: As a child, Denise loved school and dreamed of one day becoming a teacher. The challenge of learning excited her, and as she went on to study education in college, so did the challenge of teaching. Denise married and soon began working with fourth graders in a somewhat underfunded district. Making do with outdated textbooks, she learned that "the teacher was more important than the materials."

After taking a 16-year break from teaching to raise her three daughters, Denise enrolled in a master's program and soon returned to teaching after receiving her degree. She went on to receive her administrative certificate and is now working as assistant superintendent of a small suburban district.

Denise's Advice: Never quit working toward your goal. If you love this profession, stay with it until you reach the top. Remember: It's never too late, and nothing's impossible!

Rachel: Being the oldest in a family of nine children, Rachel grew up with much responsibility. That kind of background gave her the "take charge" attitude that has helped make her successful today. Currently working as an assistant superintendent in the South, Rachel is married and has one son. She began her career as a fourth-grade teacher, then went on to work as an assistant principal. After receiving her college degree, Rachel obtained two master's degrees—one in administration and one in supervision.

Rachel credits her many mentors, including her active 92-year-old aunt, for giving her the courage to continue in her career path. Even though her gender has brought on many problems in her profession, Rachel has overcome them to be a success.

Rachel's Advice: Remember that you *make* things happen. Don't be afraid to try something just because it's not "traditional" for women. You can be anything you want to be! Always strive to improve yourself and never stop learning.

Lesson 1: Be Prepared

You will need the necessary tickets but the tickets do not guarantee you a position.

—Diane

An obvious requisite for ascending to top administrative positions in education is being prepared. In a 1990 research project sponsored by the U.S. Department of Labor, Women's Bureau, it was reported that although women have been in the labor force for a significant number of years, are more highly educated than ever, "have the necessary technical skills to succeed . . . and occupy about one-third of all management positions, they are still clustered in the lower levels of management in positions of authority, status, and pay than men" (Scandura, 1990, p. 6). The problems for women are not the formal, tangible barriers, such as education or certification, but the intangible, informal ones that require an aspirant to be accepted as "one of us" by those already at the apex of the organization (Lynch, 1990).

In surveying women administrators who had achieved their goals and reached top-level positions in educational administration, the advice mentioned by them most frequently was "be prepared." Typically, "preparation" includes having the necessary degrees and credentials that qualify one for a position of leadership. Certainly, this is a must. Catherine's experience validates the need for credentials:

Throughout my career I have been hampered by the lack of degree, not the lack of skills or experience. The salary initially set for the position was commensurate with the duties, but because of the education limitation, the board was unwilling to pay the appropriate salary.

Catherine eventually achieved her high-level position as Assistant Superintendent, Business Services, but not without working twice as hard to prove herself. Other respondents, however, did mention that just having the degrees and the credentials didn't fulfill all of the preparation criteria. Diane said it well when she stated, "You will need the necessary tickets but the tickets do not guarantee you a position," thereby implying that one must have the necessary credentials to get in the door of educational administration, but once in, there was no guarantee that those credentials would provide one with actual access to a position.

The respondents indicated further that an aspiring female administrator must receive her professional training at a prestigious university and needed to engage in ongoing professional development. Although the number of women receiving doctoral degrees in educational administration has increased considerably since the 1970s (from 20% in 1972 to 55% in 1991), women educators, like women in other professions, have a considerable distance to go toward making similar gains in securing executive positions in the workplace (Gupton & Slick, 1994). So, having the proper credentials is only a part of being prepared for the jobs at the top, and it in no way guarantees acquiring a position for which one may have worked hard to attain. Even after acquiring all the credentials needed to be an administrator, Elizabeth encouraged women aspiring to be educational leaders to "read, read, read, and always strive to know more than we ever thought was possible in order to find the right [educational] match for children."

Several of the women responding to the original survey shared comments that indicated that another critical aspect affecting their ascent to the top was political awareness of the system and how it functions. Freda shares how the lack of political prowess can be one's downfall:

I am well aware that my political naivete created problems for me—that I clearly did not have the backing I needed of some key players. For this, I must look at how I did not meet up the political challenge. The shame, however, is that I truly was working wonderfully well with the teachers, parents, and administrators. Wonderful things were happening for kids in the district as a result.

Freda's experience points out the reality that despite professional success as a leader, which may be positive for the children and the district personnel, if an administrator is not politically astute, all may be lost, including the administrator's position in the district.

Another aspect of political naïveté is not being prepared for handling harassment by abusive superiors. Several of our women respondents shared incidents that revealed their naïveté with such unfair treatment. For example, Rachel tells of a particularly harassing experience she had and how unprepared she felt to deal with it:

In a northern state, I was assistant superintendent for six years before coming here. That was an interesting situation. I was forced out by a new superintendent. He had never been a superintendent. He was younger than I was, and he came to the position of superintendent from an assistant superintendency. When he arrived, he really knew how to do my job and he spent a lot of time telling me what needed to be done, in a very abusive way, too. He would like to scream and point his finger, and be very aggressive and hostile.

I had never had to deal with that, so it was very different for me. I would try to leave when he would show that type of behavior and he would say, "Sit down! You can leave when I get through!" There was no talking to him when he was in one of these moods. I really questioned whether he was mentally healthy. His mother was institutionalized with Alzheimer's and I had suggested that maybe he needed some assistance—that this was not a normal type of behavior.

We lasted three years together and he forced me out by evaluating me unsatisfactory. We had joked in the office: "Well, he can't come after me because my performance is exemplary." That's exactly the way he went after me—saying that I was unsatisfactory, and there was absolutely no way to have a rebuttal. You could discuss the differences, but when someone is intent on getting you out of there, I learned that the best thing to do is to get out.

His abuse has been a really hard thing for me to get over, because I had no control and could not do anything about it. Something was done to me that I could not stop, and it was just so frightening and scary.

What I learned from that experience was that if you're going to shoot at the king, you better kill him. As I tried to tell the board—particularly the chairperson—what was going on with our new superintendent, it all backfired on me because it came out that they were best friends. . . . I really never have gotten over that, because I believe that things that aren't fair shouldn't be allowed to go on. I am quite a naive person and one of the things that this incident did was to open me to the realities of life. I needed that, because you cannot be an effective school administrator and be as naive as I was.

From the following comments, it is apparent that it is not enough to be aware of the usual political dynamics of the system, but as women, these respondents indicated that they had to be more sensitive to the political arena's perspective of women.

Find out who is in power and is most influential in making promotions, then make sure that person knows you and your accomplishments.

Know the power bases in the organization and the community.

Put yourself in a system that will give women the opportunity to advance.

I simply had to be much better prepared than male competitors.

Unfortunately, even though one of our women was fully prepared and credentialed for the position she obtained, she subsequently learned the real reason she was hired. Elizabeth related in her story that all of the supervisors' positions until that time had been held by men. I was the first woman to apply. When I got the job, the curriculum director told me that I had gotten the job because I was female, and they were afraid the Office of Civil Rights would become involved if they didn't have at least one woman among the five or six supervisors.

What a way to start a new position. I suppose we could say, hooray for the Equal Employment Opportunity Commission, but it does not do much to help a person feel positive about the job or the people with whom she will work.

It seems that preparation for a woman to obtain an administrative position is multifaceted and not always equitable. The "preparation" to which the respondents referred also encompassed psychological aspects. Nuances of expectations of women's performance in executive positions in the profession, from the experiential perceptions of the women leaders in the profession, were that the playing field was different for them. Psychologically, in their opinion, women must be prepared for challenges above and beyond what might be expected of their male counterparts. As a high school principal, a position normally held by a male, Emily discovered an unexpected wrinkle that required some closer analysis and psychological perseverance:

> I expected some of the faculty women to like me, and, maybe even enjoy having a woman in leadership. (Remember, this was in the mid-seventies.) What a shock it was to find no loyalty and little support. The counselors and the assistant principal were terrific, but many of the teachers were, it seemed, not inclined to accept leadership from a woman. And the women teachers were less inclined. I grew up thinking that if I just worked a little harder, things would work out fine. I worked harder—and harder.

Personal sacrifices with spouses and family members are not uncommon as women strive to achieve their career goals. Spending longer hours on the job, robbed of time and experiences with children and husband, the aspiring woman professional sacrifices her personal relationships and sometimes her health to reach a top administrative position. Even so, women are expected to produce more, to prove their worth, and give more of themselves and their time in the male-dominated world of professional administrators. Volunteering for extra work and responsibilities to show their capabilities, which means longer hours at work, seems to be a requisite. As Catherine says, "Women do have to work harder and do more, and put up with more and be nicer and show more respect and not swear as much as men and not show emotion and never cry and never raise their voice in a meeting." Being psychologically prepared to handle the long hours and the personal sacrifices therefore becomes a prominent aspect of being prepared.

Brenda views her ascent to the top as a challenging journey. She states:

> My journey to superintendency was really like a climb up a tree in the forest where on each branch of the rung I gained more and more insight into my own family and psychological history as well as insight into the changing cultural milieu around me. My journey was both personal and transpersonal, psychological and sociological—of course, that's what journeys are. When I reached the superintendency I told people it was my very own "outward bound" experience. I encourage others to take the journey as I did. Prepare well, jump in. Life can be exciting and fun, if it's not taken too seriously. Leadership and modeling are about being a learner.

Of all the stories shared by our respondents, Diane's story seems to place the most emphasis on "being prepared." Although she includes other aspects that we address in the book, we felt her story was the best example of "being prepared." So here is Diane's story:

Diane's Story

> I was raised knowing that I was expected to get a college education. I also knew that upon marriage, I was on my own with my husband. I married the day my husband graduated with his 4-year degree and I received my 2-year degree. Our first goal was to get him through graduate school as he was

in education and one must have advanced degrees to progress in education. Our first child was born a year later on the day of his finals for his master's degree. He went to his test and I took a cab to the hospital (within his knowing). Our last child was born the day my husband began his internship for his doctorate.

As he was finishing his doctorate degree, I by chance began teaching, commuting 120 miles daily to finish my bachelor's degree, [then] graduated and began to pursue a master's degree, again with a commute. As that was finished I immediately began to work for principal credentials, finished that and proceeded on to the doctorate level.

I have always commuted to school and until my last job, commuted to work. It can be done. Our children all have a strong value for education (they have all graduated) and have also witnessed a very strong work ethic from their mother and their father.

In her responses to the first survey, Diane shared that she has three children, ages 30, 28, and 22. Her husband is currently a college president.

The final culmination was for me to be hired by my original school district and the one where I have lived for 30 years. I was hired as district superintendent. The following year, my husband was promoted from assistant to the president of our community college in our same town.

I am a leader who happens to be female; I am not a feminist. I do not believe in the flag raising, the high pressure tactics to further the gender. For years, I was the token female among area administrators. That is not quite the case anymore. I believe that the female characteristics that I do bring to my job include: paying close attention to detail, working with others from a "feeling" approach, having the ability to show my staff the ups and downs in this field, and being a true action person rather than just an analyzer.

Highest moments (in my career) include: students or other staff members explaining to me that I have been a true role model for them, my children using me as a role model, exposing students to the marvels of Europe, planning and initiating programs, being hired as a superintendent of my home district where I entered education as a grown woman.

My lowest moments come in this job as superintendent when I get at odds with an employee, having to dismiss an employee, or having to temporarily remove an employee from the classroom because of a substance abuse problem, and expelling students.

My role models have included an advisor in college, my husband, a college professor, and one of my elementary teachers. As an administrator, my superintendent boss when I began as a principal has been the strongest mentor and sponsor for me. I now work daily with him in an area educational cooperative.

The characteristics that Diane mentioned that were exhibited by her role models in her earlier survey included knowledgeable, supportive, hardworking, sense of humor, and goal oriented.

In giving her advice to women aspiring to be administrators, Diane related,

You will need the necessary tickets but the tickets do not guarantee you a position. You will not get every administrative position for which you apply. Especially in administration, the person must fit the current need and type of manager for the specific position. Not choosing you does not necessarily reflect negatively for you. You must earn respect by deed. You will not benefit yourself by pushing and shoving. People will expect more from you as a female leader.

If I had been five to ten years younger when I finished my doctorate and been a superintendent for several years, I would have gone into law. We need more lawyers who know the law but also realize the restrictions and arena of public education. As with conditions as they exist now—I probably would not be any happier doing anything else than what I do today. This job, however, is for the most part a lose, lose situation.

I am working to provide more balance in my life if I am going to continue as a school superintendent. I am working on my physical and mental health as well as trying to lead as well as keeping abreast of the exciting changes that are occurring in education. It is vital that good people stay in education and not be too discouraged by all the negatives. The greatest positives are the young people who really want and deserve their chance at learning.

Diane's story demonstrates the preparation and planning necessary for a person to reach her goal of becoming an administrator. Both she and her husband carefully prepared themselves for leadership options in the profession. They did so in a very calculating, seemingly predetermined manner. Diane, however, is an example of what many of our women experienced: putting their career on hold to support their husband's career. Even though she obtained the necessary credentials to secure an administrative position in the profession, she sublimated her own professional goals to those of her husband's. Had she not done so, she might have realized her dream of becoming a lawyer for public education. However, just as Diane says, having the tickets doesn't necessarily mean that you get the job you want, and in her case, she still needed more credentials to achieve her ultimate goal.

Diane also mentions the need for a careful match of the person with the needs of a particular administrative position. She alludes, with the statement about the "lose, lose situation," to the tentative security of the position and perhaps to the loneliness at the top that can occur when one is in the top administrative position of a district.

In her advice comments from the first survey, she states, "You will have to be better than your male counterpart." Perhaps she is alluding to not only the distinct need to be well prepared but also a different level of politics that affects a woman who aspires to a top-level administrative position. It seems that Diane is saying that working hard and having the credentials will get you just so far as a woman. It is implied that the next measuring stick is being as good as a man. However, to obtain or maintain your position, and perhaps even to be considered for a position, you must be better than your male counterparts.

2

Lesson 2: Plan for *Your* Career

First, my best advice is to pursue your own dreams—don't sacrifice for someone else.

—*Catherine*

This lesson rang loud and clear among the advice and lessons offered from the women in our study. Unfortunately, the majority of them learned the importance of career planning by *not* having done so themselves—a common characteristic of women who are now in their 40s and 50s. Catherine, 47, a deputy superintendent, is typical of many women her age who failed to plan for their own careers but instead provided major support for their husbands to establish careers:

> As I reflect on the past 27 years, the first thought that comes to mind is that I never intended to be a "career woman." When I was only nineteen years old, I married a bright, young man with a great future, so I left college after two years and took a cost-accounting position to help out while he completed his degree.

After several years of marriage, however, she found herself—like so many women—divorced, with no college degree, and a son for whom she provided sole support. Even though Catherine is now very successful, she continues throughout her story to refer to the obstacles created by her lack of career planning and by not having a degree:

Throughout my career I have been hampered by the lack of a degree, not the lack of skill and experience. . . . The saga continues—the position of Business Manager, to whom [I] was to report was open. The Board did not find a satisfactory candidate, and the position remained open for a year while I fulfilled the necessary duties under the title and salary of the [subordinate position]. . . . The district chose to hire a retiring army officer, with obviously no school experience. . . . Instead of fighting back when told I couldn't apply for a position I had been handling for a year, I took the traditional, subservient role, backed up the new "man," and still did most of the work.

Although (and, perhaps more, *because*) Catherine lacked formal education and the degrees to facilitate the advancement of her career, her skills in career strategizing and planning were outstanding and readily evident in her story. In her advice to aspiring women administrators, she offers good career strategy by suggesting that

early in [your] career it is important to put in extra time, develop [a] strong experience base—*never* hestitate to do jobs that men wouldn't do—you'll get more knowledge of organization and become more valuable. [The] best way I found to learn all about school business was to do every task that was needed.

This story has a happy ending as Catherine tells of the local newspaper article announcing her appointment as the "highest ranking *female* public agency employee in the county" and adds:

This is big news in an agricultural, central valley community where traditional roles and values are still relatively strong. The Superintendent has confided in me that he did have to defend his decision to hire me, given the fact that I did not have a degree. . . . I would be wrong to say that I didn't have to work very hard to prove myself during the first two years, but he recently told me that if more of his managers accepted criticism and advice as well as I, his job would be a lot easier.

Catherine's perseverance, hard work, on-the-job strategizing, and no doubt "sheer brilliance" to boot ultimately landed her a top-level administrative position. But make no mistake, without these compensating characteristics, she is not likely to have been so successful with no formal preparation except for a high school diploma. Catherine's story is truly rare and one of beating the odds— gender and otherwise! One wonders how different her story might have been—with her sterling qualities and abilities—had she focused on *her* career early on instead of—or at least along with—helping her "bright" young husband enhance his career potential with the distinct advantage of a degree.

Many of our study's women respondents, similar to Catherine, put their spouse's careers ahead of their own. Their survey responses and stories are riddled with comments bearing striking similarity in their self-sacrificing experiences.

There were those survey respondents, however, who, unlike the majority, were sure of themselves and their career goals at an early age. They planned their careers and used strategizing skills effectively from the start throughout their careers to advance to executive-level positions. For example, Delores's story embodies the planning and career strategies recommended by most of the respondents in our study as important lessons they had learned, albeit the hard way, many times. Delores, an assistant superintendent of a middle-sized rural district, tells how she became interested in teaching as a child and took advantage of opportunities to grow and learn in preparation for a career:

> During my elementary education, I attended a two-room rural school house in Franklin, Pennsylvania. The first four grades were in one room, and then grades five through eight were in adjoining rooms. I remember being able to tutor young children as I progressed through the grades, and I believe it was at that time that I began to frame the ideal of being a teacher. When graduation from eighth grade occurred, my brothers challenged me to go to the high school to compete to be a class officer, because no one from our small country school had ever done that. Always being up for a challenge from my brothers, I decided to give that a try. So I did attend one day at the high school in the spring of my eighth grade year to campaign for vice president of the

freshman class. I was fortunate to be chosen as the vice president and that kicked off my high school career. It was a very exciting time for me, and one where I learned about new talents that I had as music and drama became very important parts of my program, even as a busy college-bound student. In my senior year, I participated in all of the plays. . . . My decision to become a teacher was completely in place as a ninth grader when I attended a career day activity and even chose the school that I would like to attend. My determination persisted and I enrolled at a state university approximately forty miles from my home to begin my courses for the elementary education degree.

Delores's story is an upbeat revelation of her many accomplishments on the path to her current top-level position. Her story is threaded with accounts of her eagerness to take on new challenges and her careful attention to adequate planning for her career advancement through formal education and a variety of positive strategies such as seeking out and learning from several mentors; extensive networking with others in the profession; and seizing opportunities to grow and learn as a dedicated, career-minded educator. The following excerpt from her story tells of her transition from a coordinator to an administrative assistant and demonstrates Delores's multi-faceted approach to career growth:

Through their [her mentors'] encouragement and their mentoring to me, I did apply for the position, and was hired to try this new administrative role. Challenges of administration were many and I took on the added responsibility of evaluating elementary and middle school principals. I decided to continue my education beyond that of workshops, inservice and courses that were offered in the area, so I chose to go to a university where I would earn my doctorate and superintendent's credentials. I reviewed many programs and chose to attend a particular university. I was encouraged by members of Delta Kappa Gamma (an educators' association for women) to apply for scholarships to assist me in the pursuit of my advanced degree. New mentors entered my life at this time and for the first time, since I began my teaching career two women were mentors for me. . . . I believe in being a lifelong learner, and I want to be a very positive role model for staff and students as we prepare to enter the twenty-first century because we will be needing to monitor and adjust our strategies and talents on a very frequent basis and will not be able to depend upon the old skills we had, but will need to continually refine and enhance our skill and expertise.

Perhaps the best example from our study's sample of a strategically planned career story is that of Gail, a superintendent of schools. Gail's story follows in its original, uncut form because, as she herself writes, "I am a classic example of how to achieve a superintendency with credibility." Here is Gail's story of success through careful planning that included thorough preparation and thoughtful selection of positions to facilitate her career advancement to attaining the superintendency:

Gail's Story

My life began in Chisholm, Minnesota, where I was born and raised. My parents had partial college educations. My father had returned after World War II and opened a business store. He had been involved in the Air Force and had learned quite a lot about electronics. Thus, when the new technology—i.e., television—came out, he was in the forefront of that. He was able not only to sell tv's, but also to repair them. I was a good student in high school, among the honor students classification, though I was not the valedictorian nor the salutatorian of my class. At the time it was time to graduate and move on with my life, I perceived myself, having never talked with a high school guidance counselor, because, of course, girls would not do that, I perceived myself as only having four different options as far as a career was concerned: I could be a secretary, I could be a nurse, an airline stewardess, a teacher and that pretty much wrapped it up. Given that choice, I didn't think there was anything to do but to leave to go to school to become a teacher. During my freshman year of college I decided to become a nun. I finished that academic year and left the postulancy, which was the first year of religious life. I had not received the habit nor made any vows, and I had decided to abandon that goal in favor of simply attending a public college and pursuing the education career. I went to a different college where I finished a music major which was a comprehensive major in the area of teaching. I taught K-12 music, I directed the plays, and I even in my last year taught 7th grade English. During that period of time, I became good friends with the superintendent and his wife and family. I had taught his daughter piano lessons and had considered throughout the last year or two going back to graduate school. My initial idea was to go back in music education, but I soon learned that the job opportunities were somewhat limited. My next idea then became administration, although I would have to say at the time I didn't know any other females that were in the field and I was unaware if even the field was a field open to me. I did reflect on that for some time and finally one day asked the superintendent what he thought of the plan. At that point in time I was presenting my goal of becoming a high school principal. He looked directly at me and indicated to me that I would be a fool if I didn't do that. That then, of course, drove me straight into a regimen from that teaching position into graduate school where I completed two years and a master's degree and two additional years of study, eventually earning a doctorate in 1984. During the last several years of those years at the university I interned as an assistant principal at an urban high school which was close to the twin cities. I accepted a position as an assistant principal in a suburban town. From that position, I received a phone call asking if I might be interested in a principal's job in a small town high school, grades 7-12 of 400 students. I indicated I was interested and went through the interview process and landed the job. I worked there three years as the high school principal. It was a marvelous experience. I spent time with three different superintendents in those three years, one that had hired me; the second one was of the old school, though we got along very well. He had an administrative style which could be described as non-participatory. He made the decisions, we acted them out. He and I for some reason, even though we were diametrically opposed in our styles, got along very well. Finally, the third superintendent that went to that district, who I believe at this time still remains there, became a good friend of mine and in fact we saw so many things in the same light that we were able to build some good things for the school district working together at it.

During that period of time there were some other significant events that took place. The summer of the last year I was there, I did complete the writing of my doctoral dissertation and also I became a mother, in the sense that I adopted an infant from India and had both the job and the single parenting to contend with. It probably, though it was a personal choice, has had the greatest impact on me professionally, perhaps even more so than all of the years of education that I have mastered. Then, I was again called and asked to apply for a principalship in another state. I got that position and I remained at that high school for two and a half years. The difference between my last two positions was, of course, primarily the size of the schools. The first had about four hundred students and the school into which I went had fifteen hundred. The years there were good in that it was the large school experience I was looking for. On the other hand, those were the years when I found out about subtle discrimination and experienced it in reality. It was very difficult to come in as a young female into a very traditional high school. There was a lot of skepticism as to whether this was the right decision on the part of the school board there to have hired me for that position. It would be fair to say that I'm proud of the job that I did in that I learned and gained a great deal and have appreciated many of the friends that I made there, including many of the parents, but I would also have to be honest in saying that I was glad to leave that position, knowing that it would be several more years of an uphill battle before I would be truly accepted.

I left there to pursue a director of curriculum and instruction job where I once again had been called to apply. When I left to go to the new positions, I not only needed to sell a house and pack up my belongings in order to move, I also brought with me a second baby, having just adopted a second child from India. So, I at this point had a four-year-old and a new baby. The years in this curriculum position were excellent in that I was able to do some of the curriculum work that I had always wanted to do. In fact, there was less night work than I experienced when I was a high school principal. That was a real plus because my children were small and I was able to spend more time with them. However, I also learned one of the great lessons about a job like that—while I was there—in that when the budget crunch came, my job was eliminated and very probably perhaps it was one of the first to be eliminated. The lesson I learned is that those kinds of jobs, though they might seem ideal, do not have the longevity and security that another type of administrative position might have. So, though I had intended to be pursuing a superintendency, I had imagined it would be one or two years down the road from when I actually found myself pursuing that position. So, as they were laying me off, I began to search for a superintendency and was fortunate enough to interview in for one. I can still remember the day I went off to that interview in that I was saying to myself something to the effect of "this is an excellent experience— this interview for a superintendency—it will certainly give a good background for when I really interview for a superintendency." Little did I know that I would be quite taken with this place and accept the position after it was offered to me and put in three years of some of the finest administrative years I have ever imagined. The years there allowed me, because of the setting being a small school district of about eight hundred students altogether K-12, to be able to pursue all kinds of interests that I had. I began a weekly column in the newspaper which I kinda divided between some school related matters and some parenting matters. I began to write in somewhat a humorous style and got quite a lot of rave reviews from the community, appreciating very much the sense that I was a parent like all of the rest of them. Also, no sooner had I moved to there, within a month, I also had my third child from India—an infant—arrive. At this point, I was beginning my superintendency with a child going into second grade, a preschooler, and a baby. I stayed in there for three years. I left, probably one of the most difficult partings that I have ever gone through in my life. Though I had tried to ink out a more secure package for myself in my contract negotiations, it was difficult to do because of a turnover on the school board and, as a result, I was finding that I was going to have to be in limbo a little longer than I wanted to. I told the board, basically, that I really needed them to do a better job or that I would have to pursue other options. I think, perhaps, it was a combination of them guessing I wouldn't do that and me saying my word is my word. To make a long story short, I made some other applications and was a successful candidate. I grabbed the opportunity, probably would never have thought of it if I hadn't promised myself I would start looking because I really was very happy where I was; but as it unfolded, it seemed exactly the right place to go. I was moving a little bit closer to the range where I was born and raised but far enough away so as to pursue my own life. I was going to be in a school district of about three times the size of where I'd been which put the district in a little bit more secure place. I perceived the educational opportunities for my children as they went through the system as much greater in the new district. And then the advantages of living closer to a large city were obvious. I have been here now for two years, and have intentions of making this my last stop prior to retirement. I'm age forty-five and I'm looking at a lengthy and positive career here the remainder of my days. Sue is age twelve and she'll be starting seventh grade, Elaine is age eight—she'll be starting third grade. Patricia is age five. She will be starting kindergarten.

Personal and Professional Landmarks

The arrival of my children tops the list, hands down. I'm very fortunate, though my children were sight unseen, with no background information; literally my name came up next on the list for whatever child was available. I was fortunate in that three out of three are not only wonderful children, but are able to carry themselves academically very well. My first two children, having already been in school, are straight A students and do well socially also. Perhaps my other professional landmarks have to do with the earning of my master's degree and my doctorate. I don't think for one minute that I got the jobs I got because I have a doctorate, but I will say that as a female, it was a lot easier for me to achieve credibility in the initial interview stage with certain qualifications in my resume. Those would definitely include my education as well as my experiences. A key series of experiences that I think have made all the difference for me have been the fact that I have pursued working up the ladder. I started with an assistant principal position, a small town superintendency and now a larger school superintendency. I think the fact that I have earned my stripes has made quite a difference.

The Highest and Lowest Moments

The highest moment, of course, hands down—the arrival of my three daughters—the going to the airport to pick them up. I can't express the excitement and the joy that they have brought me throughout the last twelve years. The fact that I never was married and had I not adopted these children would be a different person today. I can only say that I often think that my life has taken such a different turn because of these children; I know that before their arrival in my life I had important things to do, people to see, places to go, but for the life of me now, I can't remember what important things those were. These children are the total thing for me at this point. My career and my children comprise my whole life.

The layoff from my position as curriculum director tops the list of low moments. It stunned me! When I look back on it now I would have done the same thing that the school district did. When they were experiencing six hundred thousand dollars worth of cutbacks, they eliminated the director of curriculum position, as they should have. At the time, though, I took it very personally. I was very depressed about the idea that it must have been me that caused this; it must have been my inability to work hard—that sort of thing. I was very hard on myself. In reality two interesting things happened. An incredible group formed. Friends rallied around me to tell me that no one could have worked any harder, that I'm a very hard working type person. Second thing that they said to me was that sometimes when these kinds of things happen, a better situation will come about. At the time I couldn't imagine what that would be, but as I reflect back now, that all had to happen in order for me to have made the career moves I made, which brings me to the second low point and that was to say "Bye" to my district. It was very, very difficult. My very dear friends still remain there and I still, of course, am in touch with them from time to time. Another painful matter that's more personal in nature is the death of my father a year ago. It was an unusual circumstance in that he was not expected to die and it just so happened that I was going to visit him and I had taken a day off of work, left two of my kids at school and took the little one with me, went up there, had a lovely visit with my father in the morning, fed him some lunch, and then after lunch, he just slipped through my hands. I felt very fortunate in that I was there. We were very close and it mattered a lot to me to be there at the end for him.

My Sources of Strength and Motivation

I have a lot of strength and motivation within me. Lots of people marvel at how I am able to do as much as I am able to do—raising the kids and working a career as I am. Perhaps, because I was older when the children came into my life. I was thirty-three; perhaps it's because of that I've never felt slighted or I don't feel as though I don't have a life. In fact, I had many years of worrying only about myself and doing only as I pleased, so right now, the fact that I sacrifice pretty much all of my nonschool hours for my kids doesn't seem like a sacrifice to me. It is what I am choosing to do. The kids are my source of strength and motivation. I enjoy working with good people around me. They also enhance what I do. They charge my batteries and I feel as though when I have "idea" people around me and doers that I perform better. I play off of other people and they play off of me very well.

Women's Status Changing

It's changed a lot in some ways and not at all in others. When I entered this profession and went down to the university, I didn't give a lot of thought to anything except knowing I would probably be one of very few females. I didn't personally know any other females in school administration. As it turns out, I was right, though I did learn and meet a number of good people. There were some good friends that I feel at the university in graduate school that were females and to this day I cherish them—good friends. As I moved up the ladder, there were fewer and fewer females actually pursuing a career in administration. There were more females when I was an assistant principal, fewer when I was a high school principal, and a very limited number during these years that I have been superintendent. In fact, the statistics have not shown a sizeable increase in female numbers in this profession for quite a long time. I have not had difficulty relating or communicating with my peers, i.e., other superintendents which happen to be male in other school districts. I think that my colleagues have, once they have gotten to know me and have heard my past experiences, know full well that nobody achieves the level of superintendency, most especially a female, without having earned their stripes and paid their dues. It's not something you get to be—it's not an advantage to be a female. In fact, it's a disadvantage. People might be thinking that it's okay to have a female principal; but it's not necessarily an advantage to be a female trying for a superintendency. People's mindset is male in that regard and it can work to one's disadvantage if one isn't completely qualified. I think the barriers I've encountered along the way have not had anything to do with education. I've always been a good student, and so my years at the university were really barrier-free to a large degree. Even in applying for and getting jobs, I've been fortunate in having gotten several jobs where I was asked to apply for the job and I have gone to very few interviews and had no job offer. Most of the interviews I have ever gone to, I have gotten the job offered to me. The interesting things, though, have to do mostly on the job—dealing with some other male administrators, and I've encountered this in a few different locations—a male principal who has some difficulty dealing with a female and not only a female, but also a very bottom line type of person and sometimes a male who is in a position of authority under mine has some difficulty with that.

Role Models, Mentors, and Sponsors

As far as role models, mentors, and sponsors, definitely my father has always been a role model for me through my whole life. He was far more intelligent than I ever imagine to be and a very gentle type person, a person that everyone got along with. The other influence that my dad had on me had to do with incredible attention to detail and organization with regard to projects. I remember the way that he would approach one of his jobs or tasks and it has filtered over to the way that I handle things. I don't simply seek a quick solution but rather look at the problem from all angles and imagine what the multiple solution might be after I have gathered all of the information. I think heavy on a good decision. Another person who has had a great influence on me back during the early years when I was teaching was a superintendent that I worked for at the time. He and I have remained friends all these years. He has since retired from the superintendency. The years that I was there, I was a music teacher and a seventh grade English teacher. I also taught his daughter piano lessons. We became friends from the beginning of my years there and had many interesting conversations with regard to a variety of topics. I remember when I started directing the plays there, he put together a lighting system for me so that we could be able to dim the lights. His background was science and mine was more the arts at that time. When I decided to go into administration, it was along about the third or fourth year that I was in that system—it popped into my head partly in frustration over a principal that I was also working with at that time. I remember myself being frustrated by the principal's decision. One day I *kind* of very out loud said that I felt that even I could do a better job than he was doing. After I said that, I kind of listened to myself and began to imagine doing that very thing. I then called up my superintendent and friend and explained to him what I was thinking about and wondered what he might think of the idea. He looked me square in the eye and said, "Gail, you'd be a fool if you didn't do that." That was about all I needed to resign from my teaching position. Actually, first I applied at the university, was accepted, resigned from my teaching position and took off to begin studying for the administrative degree. Another person who came along at the time when I was a high school principal was the super-intendent where I was principal. Though I don't necessarily *perceive* that he and I have the same style of management exactly, we worked very well together. I felt very supported by him in that the ideas and visions that I held for that high school came to be realized because of the fact that he gave me a lot of lee-way to do the things that I wanted. He's a master at the art of delegation. I've often thought that I still don't master that as well as I wish I would. He did a good job of that, at least with regard to myself. I kept him as a friend all these years and have consulted with him a number of different times over situation issues and crises that have happened in a variety of school districts that I have been in. We worked together for about a year, but the friendship certainly has gone on longer than that.

Experiences Compared to Males

Now the section about my experiences compared to male counterparts. In lots of ways, when I look over the experi-ences that I've had to and through the superintendency, I don't think they probably were incredibly different than males also experienced. However, I will add this, that I probably am not unique; I'm sure there are males who have had the same experiences I have had. There probably are males who have had all of the experiences that I have had! I feel strongly about paying dues, and I experienced all the positions up to the point where I am right now. I feel strongly about the fact that I did have to garner all of the experiences beginning with an internship in administration, an assistant

principal, and principalships which I held in high schools
and in junior highs in large communities as well as in a large
urban setting. The years I spent as a curriculum developer
added a dimension that I would not have had, with regard
to curriculum if I had only stayed in the principalship. I felt
that when it came time for looking for a superintendency, I
had at least as much, and probably more background experience than many people have had. One of the things that I
certainly have paid the price for, but has been worth it on my
resume, has been the number of communities in which I have
worked. I have had to move many many times in order to
get all of those experiences and that certainly has been a
negative with regard to friendships and leaving behind good
friends, but it has been a positive with regard to the number
of different kinds of experiences I have been able to have. I
have been able to see problems, some of them similar district
to district from different perspectives because I either had a
different job or I saw things in a different light. I think that
has impacted on the way that I look at things today. I don't
often see one or two paths away from a problem. I am more
likely to see multiple paths that can be looked at and sorted
through. I have also had the good opportunity of being able
to call on a number of good friends in other districts when I
need advice or pieces of information. Whenever it's a personnel matter, I very typically call a colleague. I had a good
friend there who still remains a personnel director par excel-
lence in my mind. When I have a problem about a board
political situation, perhaps between board members or the
superintendent and the board, I call a friend who is a pro in
that particular area. There have been many opportunities for
me to get information quickly and thoroughly because of the
fact that I have made all of the connections over the years, so
the moving around from that standpoint added experiences
to my background. Because of the way that I approach tasks,
another thing that I had done in terms of accommodations
or compromises, if you call it that, has been always to approach every task and issue, every project in a very thorough
manner. I believe that gathering the background information, in presenting it that every possible piece that might bear
on this decision is presented in a neutral fashion. It would

not be atypical of me to imagine different scenarios that would be decisions with regard to the project or the crisis and then to weigh as I look at each potential decision, what the good points and the negative points to those might be, so as to be able to make the best decision for the right reasons.

I work very hard to listen to the other person, to make my points heard and understood, to sort through differences in communications, so as to clarify positions. I am more likely to look for the potential avenue of compromise so as to solve a problem rather than to come to loggerheads with regards to it; and then I have the ability, and everyone should, to put things behind me and go forward. I don't keep a book on people or past problems in a way that bogs one down eventually. I should probably keep more detailed accounting of certain problems that may be ongoing because they can come back to *haunt* you later, but I am more likely to let the past be the past and move on.

Advice to Women Aspiring to Administration

It always amazes me that there are so few women who choose to do this and how many really should do it. I've had the opportunity to encourage a number of individuals and have chosen to do that, though in many cases they have decided not to take this on, there is a commitment—time and energy taken away from your family. In education, of course, your summers are no longer your summers when you are in educational administration. I suppose for some of those reasons, many women choose not to do this. That's unfortunate because education would be better if they did because of the nature of the situation, it being so male oriented and so few females, it seems the only females that enter are highly skilled, highly motivated, persistent and so forth, so the quality of the women already in the field is excellent. I'm proud to be associated with that group of women. I don't think that would be honest to say about the entire population of men in educational administration. I think there are far more substandard performers in that group of individuals. Somehow it is difficult to get women to do it in the first place.

I don't approach my profession, my relations with others, my decision making, thinking of the fact that I'm a female and others might be males. Gender doesn't enter into it in my mind. I think of the best decisions that should be made. I try to put the operation, the district, the organization first and kids first and I guess I think of what the skills are that we need and of what the tasks are and who the best people are to do those things, not worrying about whether it's a man or a woman.

Regrets

I am a classic example of how to achieve a superintendency with credibility. Though I have mentioned the price I have paid in having to say goodbye to good friends, I have climbed the ladder *exactly* as the book would say one should do and it certainly has yielded exactly what I was after, so I don't think of anything in particular. I suppose in some ways I wish that my large high school principal experience would have been in my home state so I would not have lost those few years out of state with regard to retirement reasons. However, I can say that the depth of knowledge and new experience being there brought me was well worth it with regard to job performance and knowledge.

Any regrets? I regret not having had a husband to share my personal life with. I have learned to walk away from the building in which I work and to pretty much put the job behind me. I do a good job of picking up with my children and not letting the job go over while I'm at home. However, there are many times when it would be nice to share with a husband the frustrations and use a husband as a sounding board professionally and certainly personally. It has not been easy to have to juggle a job, with three small children, a home, etc. all by myself. I don't have any regrets over that. I would not have chosen a different path. I intelligently and thoughtfully chose what I did and am continuing to be incredibly pleased about that, but recognize the fact that it would have been easier, it still would be easier, if I would have somebody to help me with all of that. In terms of future career plans, I don't see myself moving any more. I specifically chose my last place of employment assuming that. It would serve me and I would serve it until retirement based on the fact that I'm not sure I could handle saying goodbye to good friends yet another time, so I look to the challenges that this district offers, which I think are many and varied and for right now, they provide all the things that I would like to do. When I left my first superintendency, I had brought the district right to the point of a bond election for a new building. They incidentally since did pass that bond and build a new high school or remodel right to the core a new high school. I kind of regret having missed that opportunity to do all of that, but fortunately I'm facing the same thing in this new district, so one of my future plans is to hopefully build a new school, possibly two in this district. Another challenge that I look for, over the years with some retirements coming, I hopefully will have the opportunity to have my own administrative team filled with people of vision, ethics, creativity, and participatory style of management. I'm fortunate in that the team I have right now is fine, but it's always nice to imagine down the road that one could actually build one's own team and make one's selection for one's self. One of my short term goals was to turn this district around financially which I feel is about a four or five year goal, and I feel I will accomplish it in about three years, so having passed an excess levy this fall with the community and bond in that regard, I'm able to pump into this district a new source of revenue which has made all the difference with regard to that so those are the kinds of things that I'm looking at right now. Down the road, it would please me greatly to fall back into some of my curriculum experiences and really put this school district on the map with regard to quality teaching and curriculum. Not that this district doesn't have the building blocks of that. I truly believe that there are some of the finest teachers and curriculum here that I have seen anywhere, but we could stand some organization of that, and then the marketing of it so that the community is well aware of what's happening. I look at those as the challenges, and I want to tell you in closing here that this was a lot of fun.

3

Lesson 3: Persevere

If anyone is truly interested in my personal account of how I made it to a top-level position in education, it is simply because of perseverance.

—Nell

In many varied forms, these women administrators emphasized the important role of *perseverance* in pursuing administrative careers. Their stories and responses made clear that these women were no shrinking violets. They were not easily discouraged and met persistent and often overwhelming obstacles with determination and optimism. Frequently, in the original survey, they offered nuggets of advice similar to the following quotes that reflected their high regard for perseverance:

Be persistent!

Do not give up! Keep pushing for the position *you'd* like to have.

Realize that failure is a necessary step to moving forward.

Go that second, third, and . . . mile.

Keep trying. Don't accept the first two "No's."

These women clearly accepted adversity as a necessary part of striving for and attaining their career goals; however, perseverance tempered with prudence was often suggested or implied in their stories and responses. In other words, choose your battles carefully and not at the risk of sacrificing your sense of well-being or draining yourself of positive energy and incentive.

We asked all 150 respondents to describe major barriers they experienced along their career paths at these critical points: (a) choosing a major area of study or career; (b) obtaining the necessary degree or training; (c) securing a job after college—in education; and (d) advancing their career. In addition, we asked them to describe their experiences with (e) balancing family and career, and (f) encountering gender-related barriers in pursuing their career goals, in particular. The following sections describe their responses to each of the six sections as well as include samples of the respondents' most poignant and representative comments.

Choosing a Major Area of Study or Career

Time and time again, respondents who said they had encountered obstacles at this early stage of their careers (45%) indicated the major problem at this time in their lives was either not knowing about or not being encouraged to pursue careers not traditionally occupied by women:

I really had limited information early in my life about career options. [Assistant superintendent]

Wasn't aware of careers other than education. Didn't have mentors. [Assistant superintendent, urban district of 26,000 students]

While an undergraduate, there was little encouragement to pursue anything other than earning a bachelor's degree, marriage, and teaching. [High school principal]

Started out in math but got little support or help in this male-dominated field. [Principal]

Few role models from which to base a career. [High school principal]

My own limitations in realizing what I could do. Teaching was acceptable for a woman. [Assistant superintendent]

I received limited introduction to choices—teacher, nurse, secretary! [Superintendent]

My dad was apprehensive about my choice of secondary teaching rather than elementary. He wondered whether I could discipline high school students. [High school principal]

University counselors were not supportive of non-traditional female roles in '60's. [High school principal]

Limited options for females in college in the 50's. [High school principal]

I was told by two men (one in high school and one in college) that I would not be successful. A third college advisor would not place me for student teaching. I got a new advisor—a woman. [High school principal]

The majority of respondents (54%) either stated that they had experienced no major obstacle at this point in their careers or made no response to this item. Typical of those who indicated that they had experienced no problem in choosing a career is the comment made by one assistant superintendent in the Southeast: "No problem. I've always loved education and people." However, many of the women who listed barriers early in their careers focused on their *entry into administration* after having taught for many years. It seemed, for them, choosing a career in education was not problematic, but choosing to pursue a career in administration presented a number of new career barriers:

All the college instructors in school administration were male. They strongly recommended I take another career path. [A 51-year-old superintendent of a rural district]

So few women in my courses . . . mostly directed at good old boys. [High school principal]

When I first enrolled in administration in this rural area, I was one woman among many men. No one took me seriously. [An elected superintendent of a district in the Midwest]

Not many women in administration completed guidance certification to go through back door to get into administration. [47-year-old superintendent in a district where no woman has previously held the position]

These are only a representative few of many responses indicating the problems these current female leaders in education dealt with as they embarked on administrative career goals. The discouragement experienced by these outstanding administrators at the outset of their careers juxtaposed with their present positions of power and accomplishment is pure irony! One has to wonder what these women would have achieved had they been the beneficiaries of counseling, mentoring, diversity in occupational choice, role models, and positive support in the preparation phases of their careers, either as undergraduates choosing careers initially or later as experienced educators pursuing entry into their profession's administrative arena. Indeed, the "woman's profession" has often not nurtured those who supposedly lay strongest claim to it! The label has been too loosely applied to the whole profession, when in fact it references women's proliferation only within classrooms where they have been typecast as most naturally belonging: working with children, not making organizational decisions.

Obtaining the Necessary Degree or Training

Half of the survey respondents reported having problems at this stage of their careers. Not surprisingly, the obstacles mentioned most frequently were the scarcity of time and money, and heavy family responsibilities. One assistant superintendent and mother of two children ages 14 and 19 wrote, "[The] family suggested I was neglecting the children." A superintendent of an urban district reported, "I made choices based on having job security as a wife and mother."

Still another, a high school principal, stated that she "worked fulltime, carried responsibilities of a home and family" in obtaining her PhD. Many of the respondents described their financial plights as major obstacles. An assistant superintendent in a large urban district said, "I had to finance my education. I worked 40 hours a week with a full load of classes." Another typical response was that of a principal, "My problem was finding money! I went all the way through with scholarships, loans, and my own earnings."

Some of the women in the study indicated additional problems that included long distances to drive to a university, inconvenience of class schedules and course availability, and problems coping with attitudes of male professors of administration. "I changed from administration into curriculum for my doctorate because of the degrading attitudes of the male staff in administration toward women in general," commented one of the surveyed women, an assistant superintendent of curriculum. And another wrote, "I was given more difficult assignments and asked to serve as recorder in every college class and project while working on my administrative degree." One respondent complained, "I often was given a lower grade than practicing administrators."

Obviously, these women persevered in the face of multiple problems and scarce resources to go on to achieve career success in administration. Their strength and courage are remarkable. No doubt the tempering they endured in pursuit of their career goals prepared them well for succeeding on the job.

Among the other half of respondents in the study who indicated no obstacles in obtaining their degrees, most simply state "None" or left the item blank. It is difficult to determine whether these respondents actually had no major problems in pursuing their degrees or if they simply did not have time to respond to this more tedious, open-ended part of the questionnaire. A few explained that they had been fortunate and had experienced good support more than obstacles. An assistant superintendent wrote, "I had no problem [in obtaining the degree]—actually received great support from husband who was also in grad school. And a mentor was very helpful." This overtly positive response to the item was certainly atypical, however, but refreshing and encouraging.

Securing a Job in Education After College

For the majority of respondents in the survey, this phase of their professional careers—entering the profession as teachers—was the least barrier laden. Sixty-three percent of these women administrators reported no difficulty in securing their first teaching positions. Many of them commented on how easy it was for them to secure a position. One wrote, "I had the job before my BA was finished." Another said, "Sixties were easy times for teachers!" A current superintendent in the South perhaps most accurately summed it up best for the majority of women educators in her response to the question: "Females have always been sought as TEACHERS." But for 37% of the respondents, problems existed even at this point in their careers.

Some of the respondents had gender-related problems such as the assistant superintendent who said, "I could not get a job in history, my major. It was too male-dominated," or this current assistant superintendent with a special female concern who related, "I was pregnant when I graduated so I didn't get a teaching position until January. I've had no problem since then."

Others mentioned limitations imposed by their husband's employment and the need to comply with their husband's career needs as a priority. For example, one respondent wrote, "I was restricted by my husband's career moves." Another similar response was, "I had difficulty finding a job in the area to which we had just moved in another state." Inability to relocate to pursue their own careers posed a problem for quite a few respondents; most of them did not elaborate on the reasons for immobility, but those who commented referred to their responsibility and obligation to their husbands and family.

Although securing a teaching job after their initial graduation from college was less problematic than pursuing administrative careers for these highly successful educators, the fact is that more than *one third* of this select group of talented, achievement-oriented women experienced gender-related barriers even at the *entry* level of the profession.

Advancing in Career

The survey respondents had plenty to say about the barriers encountered in this phase of their career history. Fifty-seven percent related having problems at this point. Most of the barriers they encountered as they tried to advance within the education profession clustered around three themes: discrimination against women, family responsibilities, and mobility problems.

Their remarks about the *discrimination* they had experienced were direct and to the point. The following are a few testimonials representative of many from the survey:

> I've felt that I would have gotten the superintendency had I been male. [Assistant superintendent]

> Two years prior to being selected assistant superintendent, an individual was hired largely because the male superintendent wanted a "male friend" in the central office. [Assistant superintendent]

> Had to leave the district I was in to be able to advance. The district is still anti-women in administration—the board, not the superintendent. [High school principal]

> My district always had men in administration and I never really considered that as an option for me. [Principal]

> Good old boy network. [Assistant superintendent]

> When I was completing my administrative internship, I was told by my superintendent that I had excellent potential, but that the district would never hire a woman for central office administration! Ten years later they still haven't! [Superintendent in the West]

> Males do all the hiring. [Principal]

> Being female. [A comment often repeated by respondents]

> Most jobs were open only to males in administration. . . . "Can a woman handle discipline?" . . . Wow! When I got to the interview, I did well. My initial orientation was secondary—many rebuffs. [Assistant superintendent]

It became obvious early on that I simply had to be much better prepared than male competitors; so I made sure that I knew more and produced more! [Superintendent]

The school business is still a man's world in administration. Most superintendents are men and do not feel comfortable working with a woman who is quick, smart or has more degrees than they. Women are not included in the "good ole boys" tobacco chewing sessions at the gym or fieldhouse or on the golf course. It's lonely and we are often not included in fun, relaxing things. [High school principal in Midwest]

Comments associated with *family responsibilities* were significant as barriers to career advancement and included the following exemplary remarks:

Married to a farmer and there are not many job openings in our area. [Principal]

Getting in job market after 9 years raising children. [Associate superintendent]

Divorced and responsible for two teenaged children while I earned an EdS. [High school principal]

Closely related to family obligations was the next group of comments that dealt with *mobility or lack of it*, both of which centered primarily on family and the husband's career taking priority over the woman's career:

Moved too many times early in my career to follow my husband. [Superintendent]

Only that I moved around alot to accommodate my husband's advancements in school administration, so I was "probationary" for 9 years in 3 different districts. This, of course, also affected my salary. [Principal]

> Had to commute to first and second administrative positions for seven years (30 miles one way for 5 yrs; 60 miles one way for 2 yrs.) [Superintendent]

> Mobility, the lack of it, has held me to this county. Even after my divorce my children didn't want to move. [Assistant superintendent]

Less often mentioned but still of importance coming from such a small but well-targeted representative group of women administrators were comments about not understanding politics and the bureaucracy as detriments to advancing in their careers. Also mentioned by several women in this section was the impediment they experienced because of so few mentors, networks, and opportunities to "gain good experience that would help in future positions." One minority administrator wrote candidly about her problem being what she felt was a "token appointment" and consequently being routinely left out of the power structure and important decisions of the system.

The majority of survey respondents who fell into the 43% who reported no barriers in the advancement of their careers either left the item blank or wrote "none" in the space provided on the questionnaire. Typical of those few who chose to respond more specifically are these comments:

> Once I started on the path [to administration], things have flowed pretty smoothly, I didn't always get the job I wanted, when I wanted it, but the jobs I did get were the right "fit." [Assistant superintendent in the Northwest]

> None. I have been recruited for every position I've gotten. [Superintendent]

> I never experienced any problem. I worked hard, was effective, thus was recognized. [Assistant superintendent]

There seemed to be no geographic pattern to ascribe to those who had and those who had not experienced barriers in advancing their careers. Further research is needed to provide insight into why some women among today's leaders had so many problems while fewer, but still a significant number of them, claimed to have had none.

Balancing Family and Career

This item scored a full 67% of the survey respondents who indicated they experienced obstacles in balancing family and career. Of all the items related to career barriers, respondents wrote more and used more stressful language in their responses to what obstacles were presented when trying to balance family and careers than for any other item in this section on career barriers. Some of the respondents related the following:

> This has been difficult. My husband and I have been married for 20 yrs, and have one 13-yr-old son. I have stayed up late to do chores and study or gotten up early to avoid letting my career requirements encroach on family time. I hope to graduate with my doctorate in ed. administration in May '93. I've balanced for many years. [38-year-old high school principal]

> Always a battle, even with a supportive spouse and kids that pitch in, hold their own and were good, relatively problem-free people! [Assistant superintendent with three children]

> Very difficult. . . . I completed my B.S. degree and took care of our home and 3 children. Obtaining my M.S. degree was more difficult because we lived 105 miles—one way—from the college and I had a full time job teaching. [Superintendent in Midwest]

> Impossible. [Superintendent with two children]

> This is an on-going struggle. [Assistant superintendent with no children]

> I have suffered here greatly. I am divorced and struggle to keep my children with me. I've remarried but it's still hard. [Assistant superintendent with four children]

The stress and pain are evident in these poignant responses to the question of balancing family and career commitments. Many of our surveyed women administrators chose to delay their careers until they had raised their children (which helps to explain why the average age of women administrators is several years older than their male counterparts):

> My children were out of high school before I started into administration. Increased salary helped with college expenses. [High school principal with two children]

> I have always taught fulltime, but I delayed my doctoral studies until the children were grown. [Principal with two children]

> None—family was nearly grown before I began my career. [Assistant superintendent with two children]

> What balance? I stayed home. [Superintendent with three children]

> My best years came after my children were older. [Assistant superintendent with two children]

> I did not pursue upper level positions until my children were grown. [Superintendent with four children]

Then there were the comments of those respondents who felt that their husbands presented a major concern as they pursued advanced careers:

> This [balancing family and career] is extremely difficult, especially with a traditional husband. [Principal with two children, divorced once and remarried]

> Husband has some difficulty in adjusting to my job requirements of time, which is more than his job requires. [High school principal, married once with no children]

> Terrible on my husband. He took a psychological backseat to my success. [Principal, married once with two children]

Divorced husband. [Principal, remarried with one grown child]

On the brighter side, almost one third of these highly successful women offered no remarks about balancing family and careers, and among those who did, there were some positive, upbeat responses to the obstacles presented them, such as the following:

No problem. Three children. Supportive husband. Parents helped. Husband was principal and coach. [Superintendent]

This wasn't a problem for me. [Superintendent, married for second time, with two children]

No problem since I have no children. Husband is very supportive and willing to move if necessary for my career advancement. [Assistant superintendent]

We have 7 children. It has been a challenge! Supportive husband, older kids made it work. My child care has always been done by a friend with kids of similar ages. My husband put his career as secondary most of the time. [Assistant superintendent]

I just did it—one child and a very supportive family. [Principal]

The picture is not as bleak as it could be. There are those successful women who seem to be proliferating in executive positions who feel that they have managed—usually with the help of supportive others—to balance family and career responsibilities and to be comfortable and secure and amazingly (compared with most women) guilt-free about their accomplishments. Perhaps this is what Naisbitt understood was happening when he predicted that the 1990s would be the decade for women!

Encountering Barriers That Were Gender Related

Although gender-related barriers were often mentioned in many of the preceding career phases, this item was added to solicit more direct, current information regarding practices, policies, and attitudes toward women from the experiences and perceptions of this select group among education's highest achieving female executives. An overwhelming number (70%) indicated that they had encountered some form of gender-related obstacle in pursuing their career goals. The individual responses frequently contained not one but many accounts of discriminatory treatment because of gender. The number-one area of biased treatment was related to being given less respect and being left out of the dominant male network of administrators. The following responses are typical of the majority of remarks in this section of the survey:

The good-ole-boy, patronizing attitudes keep me from being taken very seriously.

Difficulty with older males. They hate to have a boss who is female and younger than they are.

There were many times when I was the only female in a meeting. At times I was not taken seriously if the people did not know me.

The "good old boys" are alive and well. Women administrators in rural schools are treated politely by males but are not respected as equals.

Ignored by some male colleagues at meetings. When I state my teaching field as science, people condescend to "biology" teacher . . . back off when I say my master's is in physics!

Some male teachers resent a woman administrator.

Another major subset of responses to this item was most closely allied to gender-related problems created by cultural stereotypes and gender role expectations:

Belief systems that all women administrative teams can't do the job.

Females shouldn't earn $$$.

Men will never admit there are any barriers for women. Discrimination had become more subtle, but just as pervasive, over the years.

The public has received me well in the area of curriculum and federal programs, but I don't think they would vote for a woman for a superintendent. This county elects their superintendent, and women are not as respected. [Assistant superintendent]

Attitudes that women are not as good at budgets, discipline, and construction of buildings always irritates me since I have bookkeeping/budget experience and know how to design and construct houses better than many men.

Still the stereotype role of wife/mother and responsibilities around the house [exists for women].

As a woman in an administrative job, I sense that both men and women with whom I deal, parents-bosses—are more likely to push-boss me around and use anger to intimidate me than they are men who are in similar positions.

Some difficulty communicating with male parents who are used to talking "man to man" with the "man in charge."

Early on was told that I wouldn't be rehired because I was married and didn't need the money.

A third theme that emerged from the responses to the item on "barriers encountered that were gender-related" centered on the lack or inadequacy of professional networks and support systems for women:

"Good ole boy" system in administration—competing with coaches who were moved ahead.

The "good old boy" network is alive and well.

Seeking and not finding a superintendency in the _____ area. Age and gender were factors AND my *not* building a network of administrators.

Subtle—lack of support systems.

Difficult to break into the "network."

The men with whom I worked were most cooperative and helpful. Women have been somewhat less supportive.

Scarcity of role models.

Still another theme found in these women's responses to gender-related barriers was the discriminatory nature of school systems' interview, hiring, and promotion practices:

Obvious discrimination against a female in *some* districts as I interviewed.

When I applied for my first two administrative jobs, I was told I was a nice lady and they were hiring a MAN.

Interview questions were problematic but I just hit them head on nicely! . . . Young children are a real bias for a woman, in my experience. Some men can't figure how you manage (w/o a wife!). Also, the issue of my being a principal before my husband has been a side issue during interviews.

For some reason our area feels that if a woman is an administrator, she must be on the elementary level ??!

At two levels, I was prepared and applied for jobs-promotion, and male got both jobs.

Finally, some of the survey respondents looked inward and focused on their own personal problems with gender-role stereotypes or on how they had dealt with such problems:

I felt some discomfort entering a traditionally male domain.

I have not applied to a superintendency because I want to remain in the area of curriculum and instruction.

[I have encountered] many [obstacles] within my own self-perception. I grew up in the 50's.

I was mature enough to know they [gender-related obstacles] would exist, so they were not a problem. I remained focused, worked longer, harder, and ignored gender-biased comments!

Learning not to take comments to heart.

I usually ignore gender-related concerns expressed by men. If given enough time I can "win them over." I've been at this so long I can "good old boy" with the best of them!

Obviously, barriers and obstacles exist for anyone when pursuing lofty career goals. No one expects the road to be gilded or to have a crystal staircase leading to the top. However, neither should one expect to find the path loaded with land mines! The responses these accomplished women executives offered in this section concerning career-related barriers are filled with unnecessary problems created more often than not by the mere fact that they are of a particular gender. Relatively few complaints were made that did not in some way relate back to the fact that the person happened to be a female in a society that has made her gender take precedence over her competency and potential in her chosen career. The profession of education desperately needs to tap the leadership potential among its throng of women professionals to ensure that our schools have the very best guidance available. Removing stereotyped notions about who should and should not be doing the job is essential to provide the kind of leaders schools need to nurture future generations and equip them for the complexities of 21st-century living.

Nell is an assistant superintendent of schools in a southern state. Her story is one of self-professed perseverance that emerges as her number-one strategy for career success. Here is Nell's brief but interesting account of her path to a top administrative position in education.

Nell's Story

I am Nell, a wife, a mother of two daughters, and a strong champion for promoting quality and equity education to all students. Presently, I am the assistant superintendent of a school district in a small southern state.

The sources of my strength and motivation have come from a spiritual being and my family. If anyone is truly interested in my personal account of how I made it to a top-level position in education, it is simply because of perseverance.

I have especially been encouraged by the "small talk" that my mother gave me when I was just a little girl. Such small talk as "Keep your eyes on the prize, rest if you must, but do not quit" and "When given a task, whether the task is great or small, work at it with all your might." My mother was an administrator by position, but she was first and foremost a dear mother, one who taught mostly by example. Also, I have been encouraged by my husband and two other associates to remain in administration.

Therefore, my advice for women aspiring to a top-level position in education is not to give up, but to keep your eyes focused on your goal, because school business is everyone's business. I truly believe that in this business, one works with people, not for them; no one person owns a school district. We all, male and female, are in this business together and our product is the student.

Again, since I have had the position as assistant superintendent, I have been encouraged by some men and some women. At the same time, there are those who have acted as though they were not very secure with me being around. Let me reiterate the fact that it has little or nothing to do with race or degrees, it is more a lack of security, a lack of strong interpersonal skills and a vast difference in leadership style.

4

Lesson 4: Be Diligent and Professional

"Work" became synonymous with "virtue"—I developed the belief that the rewards of life come as a result of work.

Marie

Diligence

Not surprisingly, "Work hard and be qualified" were often repeated side by side in the survey responses as baseline expectations for success as an administrator. Emily tells of her rigorous schedule as a young, new high school principal in a conservative logging community on the West Coast:

My schedule was to report to my office at 5:30 a.m. I seldom left campus during the extended school day except to take a student home or to run something to the DO [District Office]. Ruth, the cafeteria manager, often sent up a lunch for me just before she left for the day at about 2:00 p.m. If she had not seen me by then, she knew I had not eaten.

I moved about the campus through the day. One teacher, complaining or complimenting, noted, "She doesn't slow down." If no event was scheduled for the evening, I would leave by 5:30 p.m. More frequently, I would go to the gym and watch a volleyball game or basketball scrimmage. I went to over 90 percent of the events whether cultural or athletic. I saw every play and every concert. I learned to enjoy all the sporting events. Often my husband and children would join me. All too frequently, dinner would be food from the snack bar grill. Twice monthly, I was at Governing Board meetings. A typical week was at least sixty hours, and usually, due to sports, more like seventy. The weeks were long and required me to be moving, moving, moving.

Like any new administrator, I had successes and failures. I worked those long hours and went to hundreds of school events seeking to become a real leader in the school.

Although no one should expect to achieve success without working for it, unfortunately this oft-repeated advice for women in the profession was sometimes accompanied by a companion perception: Women in both phases of the research frequently referred to women's need not only to have a strong work ethic but also to be willing and able to work harder than their male counterparts in administrative positions. Today's women executives, similar to those a decade ago, felt that women are still having to prove their worth (as a gender) in roles that continue to be sanctioned by the culture of the organization and by society as more appropriately filled by males. Despite a well-developed track record of outstanding performance from many pioneer women in educational administration, the "best advice" given by the 150 survey respondents included the following representative remarks:

Excel in your work.

I made sure that I knew more and produced more!

Do whatever you do well; don't be afraid to do more and to take on more responsibility.

Women can lead just as well as men, but they must work much harder to get to the same level.

Do the best job possible and respect will come.

Be the best you can be.

Prove your worth! Men don't always need to do this; just being a male is sufficient!!

Emily's story vividly demonstrates the double standard she encountered with the work expectations for her as the first female principal of a high school in a district unaccustomed to and unprepared for a woman in that position:

It was exciting and difficult for a young woman principal. The faculty was mostly male. . . . The faculty culture was male. . . . I grew up thinking that if I just worked a little harder, things would work out fine. I worked harder—and harder.

Ultimately, however, Emily's diligence on the job could not prevail over the barriers she faced as a woman in a position that had heretofore been occupied by men only. She continues:

Several times cartoons with biting labels about women in leadership or attacking my religion were found on the teacher bulletin board. . . . After my first year, although I did not know it yet, the move to have me out of the school was well underway. Years later, several people told me the superintendent had said I would only be there a year to solve the OCR [Office of Civil Rights] problem. My reports were returned with commas and other superficial grammatical corrections, even though the "corrections" were style comments and not errors. Other, less literate principals were not given this special attention. . . . Different standards of performance were expected of me than from my male colleagues and different perks were given. Wives of administrators were hired by the district if they held teaching credentials. My husband applied and was not hired. The rumor was that we did not need the second income. Another rumor was that it just was not right to have a woman making more than her husband in the district. . . . Vacations were interesting too. . . . I was not to leave without having the plant "covered" just in case. Other principals left for periods of time without the same proviso. . . . The ground upon which I stood was soon sodden and unstable. "If you were not a woman and a Mormon, this would not be happening to you." The superintendent actually said that to me! He also told me I was an excellent administrator, but he did not have confidence in my ability to be firm and to lead in that school. He said he did not need to have any reason other than that to replace me.

Although working hard and excelling on the job were clearly perceived as "musts" to advance in this profession, not one of these successful women administrators indicated that diligence and dedication alone were usually sufficient to achieve top-level positions in education for women. The "hard work" advice was always coupled with other, more strategic suggestions, many of which related to the nurturance and development of a number of critical characteristics.

Professionalism

Professionalism and strength of character along with diligence emerged as truly high priorities among these women leaders. When explaining how much she learned about school finances, management, and budgeting from one of her mentors and colleagues, Catherine, deputy superintendent, went on to say,

> More important than these [skills] was a basic tool he gave me—absolute and unwavering integrity. He was the most ethical man I ever have known. I have attempted throughout my entire working life to live up to his standards, and believe that using that principle as a guide has helped me achieve what small success I have.

Among the many comments from the original survey reflecting these women's high regard for strong, positive traits and professional prowess were the following representative selections:

Courage and integrity are the hallmarks of real leaders.

Never compromise your principles.

Be honest.

No cutesie stuff! Be professional.

Keep a professional, dedicated, positive attitude.

Be serious, be professional, but keep your sense of humor.

Remember to laugh.

Don't whine.

Don't sweat the small stuff.

Sarah alludes to these essential characteristics as well as the importance of good humor when she tells about her experiences during her first day as the first female superintendent of schools in a district. She asked the business manager to brief her on the budget; during their meeting, he said, "[Sarah], I ask only one thing of you; this is a pretty tough job and things aren't always pleasant. When things get tough, please don't cry." Sarah's response to him was, "I promise you I won't cry, but you have to promise me you won't cry either!"

Similarly, at one point in her story, Catherine wrote of the importance of diligence and the behavior expected of professional women:

> Women do have to work harder and do more and put up with more and be nicer and show more respect and not swear as much as men and not show emotion and never cry and never raise their voice in a meeting. . . . Over the past 27+ years, things have changed significantly. But the fact remains until more women are making the final decisions and setting policy on a broader scale, the world will see us as women in traditional male roles, expecting the same behaviors that have been exhibited by men, and judging their success by criteria developed by men. Unfortunately, women in supervisory roles are forced many times to apply these same criteria, thus perpetuating the problem.

Marie, a district superintendent in the Midwest, shares her full story next. Her story is presented in its entirety because we found it particularly exemplary of a woman who combined diligence and professionalism with career strategy and persistence to overcome a host of potentially career-stunting barriers to achieve success.

Marie's Story

Some people will find it amusing that the superintendent and elementary principal of a small school district in a small farming state would be described as having reached "the top." As one of four women school superintendents in my state, I am one of a select group!

When I graduated from a local university in 1954, I felt that I had made it to the top. With the help of scholarships and part-time jobs, I had a degree "with high honors," was on my way to my first teaching position, and about to be married.

I was the second of eight children of a farm family in the southwest. My parents had both left post-secondary education in the depression and started their family. They cleared 40 acres of sagebrush to begin farming, a part of changing the desert to productive agriculture. We eight children worked side by side with our parents in the field, the garden, and in the barnyard to make a living for the family and pay the farm mortgage payments. "Work" became synonymous with "virtue"; I developed a belief that the rewards of life come as a result of work.

After my junior year of high school, at the age of sixteen, I went to live with a family closer to town working as a "mother's helper." This family gave me extra chores to earn money and they encouraged me to enter the university when I graduated from high school. While at college, I believed that I owed my benefactors—those who had given me scholarships, grants, and jobs—the highest academic achievement that I could reach. I worked hard to get high grades and prove to myself and to my benefactors that I was worthy of their assistance. Thus, graduation from the university was a crowning achievement for me. I was a success. I had made it to the top!

My first teaching job was in a coastal state, where my husband was stationed in the Navy. Two years later, I followed him to another state where he went to graduate school for three years while I taught second grade. When my husband finished his training to become a Methodist minister, we moved back to the west and started our family.

We experienced the dynamics of social conflict in small towns during the 1960s and '70s. The social climate in America was seething with conflicting views on integration of blacks, treatment of Hispanic workers, the Vietnam War, and youth who wore their hair long. People encountered unfamiliar ideas, which frightened them, and they responded with tremendous emotion. Time and television eventually soothed fears, but in the meantime, people lost many of the values they had previously held. My experiences of the '60s and '70s are helpful in the '90s as a school administrator dealing with change in a small town.

When my children were in school, I returned to teaching in the elementary grades. I remember one day when I was so happy with my job, that I practically danced across the field toward home, thinking "This is the most wonderful life!" I felt fulfilled in that I could see children learning, they showed their love and appreciation of me, and the parents and school leaders appreciated my work in the classroom.

After three years of teaching, I was assigned a first grade that had four very active little boys that I could not seem to reach. I believed that there were methods to reach these children and I wanted to learn what those methods were. That was the impetus to set me on the road toward a master's degree in special education.

In 1976, armed with my new master's degree, I obtained a job as a special education resource specialist. Public Law 94-142 was new; school leaders were suspicious of the new law and the new brand of professionals it brought into the schools. Many of us special educators were assertive. We had been taught to be advocates for disabled children and our training brought us in conflict with our school principals. The new law and the new professionals, including myself, were attempting change. Our school principals were uncomfortable with, and even actively opposed to, the new requirements.

Somewhere in my first years as a resource specialist, it occurred to me, "I have some of the course work completed to be a school principal; and as a principal, I would be able to see that children had [the] opportunities they need in school." I learned that some courses in school administration were being taught in our part of the state. I signed up for one, only to learn that it was taught during the school days that teachers were working with children. It was then that I learned about the "old boy network," where attractive and promising young male administrators were "invited" by their superiors to become administrators. The members of school administration classes were already in administrative positions, while taking courses to become qualified for the job! The fact that I was an "uninvited" participant in one of their courses made me a very fractious individual in the eyes of administrators of my district, as well as those of the surrounding districts. I found that the certification rules in the state also worked against an "uninvited" school administrator. One could not renew his certification as a school principal unless he had held a job as a principal for two years.

I applied for several administrative positions in my home district but did not receive any. I was told that in order to be an administrator, I must first "pay my dues." Paying dues meant working my way up first by coaching, then to vice principal, then principal and finally to administrator— and I had never been a coach. The district apparently feared that I would file a discrimination suit. Other women had filed suits, but even when these women won the battle, they lost the war. They were stuck in impossible jobs, treated badly, and eventually eased out. Going to court was not an option I chose.

I participated in the state's Northwest Women in Educational Administration group and found great support from other women. From this group, I learned how to develop a consensus in decision making and how to be a leader without being male.

Eventually, I applied for and was offered a position as elementary principal in a small town in Idaho. I was unsure whether to take the job, because it meant moving away from my family. The district administration where I was working seemed extremely anxious to know whether or not I was going to take the other job. The moment I announced that I had signed a contract with the other school district, the district where I was at the time announced an opening for elementary principal!

My youngest child graduated from high school that year and enrolled in the regional junior college. I turned the family checkbook over to her and moved, by myself, to the new school administration job. A year later I was divorced from my husband—a predictable event with many causes, not just the result of my moving away to the new job.

For two years, I enjoyed the job of elementary principal and physical education teacher in the small logging town in the central part of the state. The town was receptive to me and to my ideas. We formed a school advisory team of staff and patrons, which instituted plans for school improvements and participated in hiring decisions. At the end of my second year, the district hired a new superintendent.

At the same time, a friend encouraged me to apply for a position in the state as an elementary school consultant. I took the job with two aims in mind: First, I would do my best to improve elementary schools in the state, and second, I would use the position to become a better educator. I believe that I was able to fulfill both of these goals in my six years as a state "bureaucrat."

While there, I worked with the elementary approval committee to make some important school improvements. I also attended national conferences and helped build and strengthen the ASCD state affiliate. I completed my education specialist degree and school superintendent certification. Then I began watching for an opening for school superintendent in a small school district. I found the position in a small logging town of about 600 people and a school with a little over 300 students in grades K through 12.

Being the administrator of a small school district in a small town is a far cry from being "at the top" of a school system like Chicago or Boston. I am comfortable. I feel more effective working hard in a small community. We are not just educating children, we are participating together with families to provide opportunities for their children.

The district where I am now is slowly becoming known in the state as an innovative school district in which school reform is not just talked about, it happens! Staff members attending summer school have to bite their tongues to keep from repeating too often: "Well, in this district, we do it such and such a way!"

As we make changes in the school, we experience the same kinds of pain that change has always brought in small communities. It reminds me of my experiences in the '60s and '70s, when people were experiencing so many changes in ideas and institutions. So far, we are moving forward by keeping patrons informed and involving them in school decisions. I recognize that tolerance for change can become saturated overnight, so I keep a watchful ear on the community grapevine.

I am not a charismatic leader, or a leader of any personal power. I am not an articulate speaker, but I am a risk taker who will attempt difficult tasks to advance toward a worthwhile goal. I am persistent in the district's mission. I have a strong value system and a rich variety of experience. I have learned much about building a consensus from my experiences and I am comfortable sharing leadership with staff members, the school board, and patrons. I credit my knowledge of consensus building to my association with other women in leadership positions.

Four of the 113 school districts in the state have superintendents who are women. None of these four women has moved from one superintendency to the next. Other women in the state who have left the superintendency have found positions in higher education, instead of other jobs as chief administrators of school districts. I suspect that women in this state will continue to find that getting their second superintendency is even harder than getting their first.

Advice to Aspiring School Administrators

Our society teaches women behaviors or skills that enable them to be different leaders from the traditional male figureheads. Women have always been able to use these skills to get things done. Now America is learning that a leader does not have to be dominant, authoritative, or male.

Moral leadership is one of the greatest challenges in American education. Establish your own personal code of ethics and apply it daily. Be willing to risk job security for maintaining your code of ethics. Men and women who aspire to leadership in education must have the strength of character to take an action because it is "the right thing to do."

Lesson 5: Honor, Preserve, and Protect Your Integrity

Personal integrity is paramount.

I promised myself decades ago that no job would cause me to violate my personal ethics. I will die upon that mountain—or I will bring others to my mountain top.

—*Emily*

Doing the right thing is an anomaly, and it costs.

—*Brenda*

M any of the women responding to both surveys either directly or indirectly alluded to the importance of maintaining one's integrity at all times. With such comments as, "Never compromise your principles," "Maintain personal ethics and values—nothing is worth losing them," and "Remember, be yourself, not what others think you ought to or should be," our respondents fervently expressed their belief in maintaining their integrity as professionals and as women. Much of the advice these women shared encourages other women to be their own, unique selves, to espouse their values and live them, and to equally respect the values of others. Another respondent states, "Being oneself, modeling what one values, and having the courage and confidence to follow one's value system are critical components to survival in the quest and attainment of top leadership positions." This is not to say that frequently one's ethics will be challenged. Emily shared this account with us in her story:

> Mr. X left angry with me. It was not the first time he had asked me to do something morally, ethically, or legally wrong. But it was the most difficult. I clearly told him I would not comply, despite his finger waving in my face.

She states further that

> I have had to reach down into my deepest resources several times in my career and demonstrate the sort of courage that could have been a front page newspaper story (but never was). Daily, I must show integrity.

In our original research, one of the reasons for aspiring to be administrators that was most frequently mentioned by our respondents was their belief that they could do something positive for children. Underlying this goal are the ethics of honesty and positive values that keep these women focused on what is "right" and "just" for children. Elizabeth expresses a common attitude of these women administrators: "I would not be able to make decisions just to keep my job when I know that the decision was not in the best interest of the students." So, it seems that if it is not right for children, these women will risk their jobs and their reputations to do what they believe is right. They express their value of integrity and advise aspiring women in the profession to safeguard their values, remain true to themselves, and never forsake their principles. They appear to be saying that a woman in a position of leadership must never stray from exemplary integrity; her conduct and values must be unreproachable. It is almost as if the woman must be perfect in morals, ethics, conduct, and principles. The female administrator has no room for error lest she be judged by the male-dominated world of educational administrators as lacking in integrity and ethics. And so it seems that once again, female administrators must work harder even at being ethical. Suffice it to say that especially in the area of ethics, the female administrator does not get to play on the same field as her male counterparts. Marie says it well when she states,

Moral leadership is one of the greatest challenges in American education. Establish your own personal code of ethics and apply it daily. Be willing to risk job security for maintaining your code of ethics. Men and women who aspire to leadership in education must have the strength of character to take an action because it is "the right thing to do."

For the past 8 years, *USA Weekend* has explored and surveyed issues related to families in an effort to track the changing concerns and values emerging in today's society. In a recent edition, November 17-19, 1995, of *USA Weekend*, the results of a reader survey indicated that *compassion, tolerance, responsibility, integrity, and perseverance* were highly valued by American families today (Fields, 1995, p. 4). These very values are the essence of the characteristics of the women leaders who are telling their stories in this book. They are leaders who value people and who involve the people they work with in the decision-making processes that affect those very people. They are women who will not sacrifice their integrity for selfish or political purposes. They are strong women who persevere through all kinds of adversity to achieve their goals because they believe they can make things "better" for children. Believing in the value of integrity does not mean that it is easy to hold on to it, especially if one is faced with situations such as Brenda's. She comments that "Honest, high values are counter-cultural (in some situations); surviving takes skill. The playing field is complex and not for the faint of heart." Brenda's story is a good example of a successful ascent to the top, but it also gives us a realistic view of the cost to get there. Reaching the superintendency in a large district took its toll, because like some of our other storytellers, she discovered that the playing field is indeed not level for all the players.

Brenda's Story

Before I start my story I must tell you I left the superintendency one month after I completed your first survey. I was making $60,000 a year. Part of the reason I left is directly related to my being a woman. There were benefits and drawbacks to being female. One benefit was that my husband of 34 years had just retired from a major multi-national oil corporation and I was not financially dependent upon the job, nor have I ever been. As a woman who grew up in the '50s, when I married my expectation was that my "prince charming" would "take care of" me for the rest of my life. I am fortunate, in that sense, because in a material sense that expectation happened. However, as I matured and individuated and the culture changed, my rising expectation also included fulfillment through my career.

One day in April 1992 I unexpectedly experienced the phenomenon of instant menopause. I had been through a lot of pressure from a principal non-renewal hearing. The principal's wife and her sisters, his brothers, intermarriage to just about everyone in the area, a long history of family local power politics, a staff of co-dependent, fused female teachers, and two special education students who were "inappropriately disciplined" and known in the community for deserving punishment were pitted against "the superintendent." In addition to my own professional indignation that he (the principal) didn't see his behavior as at all inappropriate, or report it after the police were involved, I knew the community was liable because, as a "good old boy," he had been employed by a previous superintendent. He was not even licensed to be a principal (female superintendent versus local area inbreeding and a long history of "good ol' boy politics"!).

PhD with an X through it appeared around town. I later learned that was about "the superintendent." . . . As I was an Ed.D. I didn't even get the connection at first. A woman with a doctorate who brought down a powerful good ol' boy was absolutely adding insult to injury. A petition was circulated to have the superintendent removed. Fortunately, the boards I worked for were supportive of me throughout, but the politics were particularly undermining in my own office. My secretary had gone to school with him and the business manager, payroll clerk and special education director (all women) were not functional enough to remain loyal to me. They pouted, complained at every opportunity and backstabbed. When I was out of the office the former principal would appear, and they adoringly gathered around him. Either they had to leave or I had to leave. It was just not an infrastructure I could mold to my value system without more "bodies." The many boards and responsibilities were enough challenge on their own, but the additional political shots and unsupportive office were more than I wanted to continue to battle. Lack of sleep caused by estrogen fluctuations and night sweats became more than I wanted to live with.

A few more people needed to leave to establish the new norms, but I decided to put one full year behind the incident and to pass the baton with intact boards to a new superintendent who shared my value system and could continue the movement we'd made in the district. The community culture needed to heal and hopefully move forward. (I think that is happening—my work there was not in vain.)

The lack of rational behaviors in schools and communities is not unlike the recent O.J. Simpson fans. Many people are in denial or just cannot separate people from inappropriate, unacceptable behavior. Tolerance of intolerable behavior has become a national norm. It is not surprising when leaders at any level have to face this dilemma. When they know it comes down to their own survival, the long term souls choose to ignore the obvious, become blind to it, or actively support it. Again, this is not unusual in any sphere of leadership in our country today. . . . Doing the right thing is an anomaly and it costs.

In June of 1993 there were 12 women superintendents in the state. At this time nine of those women (including myself) have left the superintendency. Some other women have come in and replaced us, but presently there are only nine women of 182 superintendents.

I was successful as a superintendent because I grew and learned at a very rapid pace during my three years in the position. I am happy and excited to share my success because I forged a path for myself—not so much to put myself to the test as to realize the benefits that level of responsibility brought to my confidence and interior growth. The job involves skills of leadership which include independence, creativity, political savvy, interdependence, decision making, breadth of knowledge, risk taking, confidence and competence. In short, a great vehicle for contribution and individuation. Developmentally, it met my needs and gave me a chance to be a role model for others, especially the children. Thus, I encourage others to aspire to the position and not become disheartened by the challenge. I learned karma lessons I needed from the job, which is one reason why I'm not needing to do it again right now. Now, developmentally my body, mind and spirit are requesting self care.

It would be easy to produce a book on this topic which totally misses what it means to have pioneered in this work because we are reflecting on our own imbeddedness in a cultural "forest." The old adage that it is very hard to see the forest for the trees is applicable. I never wanted to believe I had less opportunity than the men. I never wanted to believe the cards were stacked against me. I never wanted to believe that when push comes to shove, people can be mean, base and self-serving. I never wanted to believe people would almost kill to maintain power and control independent of right or wrong. But those were childish and unrealistic principles. At mid-life, in my case, I learned about the realities of life—this really sounds like a woman of the '50s, but it's true.

In short, I was an innocent—a girl from a rural hamlet in the northeast. My people were farmers. My father was a dyslexic with an eighth grade education and my mother had a 10th grade education. My father's father was a travel executive, and earlier in his career, he had owned a steamship company. His brother, my uncle, was a southeast Asian representative to Lockheed. My mother had been born out of wedlock to immigrant farmers. She was curiously different from her half-sisters—very sensitive, bright, regal—she had carriage and class, but it was different from the earthiness of her mother and sisters. I loved everything about her—her smell of freshly pressed powder, her soft skin, her beautiful face. She held me the many days and nights I was sick as a child and we were closely bonded, too closely bonded. She was a woman who carried deep layers of shame. She was "different"—no question she could have been a corporate V.P. if she'd been born in a different time. She always praised education—valued it deeply and wanted it for my older sister and me, especially me because she knew I was academically bright, popular, outgoing and a "fighter." Her deep sense of inadequacy and repressed anger were internalized like a marble cake within my psyche. While I acted out her achievement needs each gift I ever shared was systematically shamed and cursed. I could not run far enough ahead of my feelings of inadequacy. I inherited my mother's driving energy, verbal ability, intellectual competence and deep internal shame. The aspect of who I was which I valued the least was from my father—a simple but deep faith in God. He always modeled that faith through his beautiful singing voice and his living example of the "Golden Rule." However, any appreciation for my own "masculine" gifts from him eluded me. My sister was my father's child and I was my mother's, her alter-ego, princess, and object of her pride and projected shame. My journey to superintendency was really like a climb up a tree in the forest where on each branch of the rung I gained more and more insight into my own family and psychological history as well as insight into the changing cultural milieu around me. My journey was both personal and transpersonal, psychological and sociological—of course, that's what journeys are.

At "the top" of my personal career ladder, from 1990 to 1993, I took a good look at the terrain and made a conscious decision to move to a hill near the forest where I could maintain perspective and perhaps hold a mirror up for others to see what I had gleaned.

In August 1993, my husband and I joined a group of aspiring superintendents as superintendents in a Caribbean Seminar at Sea. My advice to new women superintendents is to network heavily. The Women's Caucus of the American Association of School Administrators was particularly helpful. It was through them that I met Sharon and Lucy—two top-notch, high-powered role models. They led the seminar. It is also crucial to have a strong support system in place while you are in the job. Daily experiences are so unpredictable, trauma can assail you at any moment. It is absolutely crucial not to let the stress and shock build up physically, mentally, or spiritually within your system. Self-care needs to be paramount to any effort to be effective in helping others.

Challenge and growth need to be one's values. Fear of change can be overwhelming. Risk-taking sounds like a cliché, but it's not a very comfortable place to be. When I reached the superintendency, I told people it was my very own "outward bound" experience. I encourage others to take the journey as I did. Prepare well, jump in. The water's fine. Life can be exciting and fun, if it's not taken too seriously. Leadership and modeling are about being a learner.

Even though it took Brenda a while to realize the hidden political and power agendas of others in the business, she never wavered in her own convictions. She did what was right for the children and the school districts she served. Understandably, it took its toll on her physically as well as emotionally. Even so, she continued to stand by what she believed was right and remained professional to the very end of her tenure as superintendent. She stayed until the district was once again settled enough to proceed with a secure path of purposeful educational integrity and achievement. This courage to proceed under heavy fire raises another critical aspect to the issue of maintaining one's integrity, and that is a strong self-esteem.

Believing in oneself essentially means possessing a strong sense of worthwhileness or self-esteem (Gupton & Slick, 1994). Women must not only act in ways that command respect because of their intellectual prowess and their enthusiastic, positive emotional state, but also display their professionalism in impeccable dress and manners. This outward as well as tangible display of a professional persona communicates to others a strong self-esteem. Some of our respondents expressed the importance of believing in oneself by saying:

Think positively; create an atmosphere of success.

Present yourself well. Smile; use eye contact. Hold your head high.

Have a positive attitude and hold your head high.

Believe in yourself.

Comments by our respondents indicated repeatedly that successful female administrators need to possess a strong, positive self-esteem that communicates to those with whom they are working that they can get the job done and can do it well. Appearance, body language, communication prowess, intellectual acuity, and experiential background, as well as knowledge of one's best style of leadership and how to use it effectively, contribute to the total perception of an administrator. According to Linda Hampton Wesson, the most important ingredient for (a school administrator's) success is honest and objective evaluation of your strengths and abilities as well as your aspirations (Wesson, 1995). She states further that this self-assessment is a continual process that helps you understand your strengths and abilities so that you can put your energies where your talents and interests are (Wesson, 1995). Self-awareness and reflective practice should be grounded in realistic self-analysis. Ongoing professional development or self-improvement is the mark of an ever-growing professional. Brenda says it well and succinctly: "Challenge and growth need to be one's values." If this attitude is accompanied by a strong self-esteem, a leader, whether female or male, will continue to develop and be able to meet the changing challenges of educational leadership.

Recently, in another issue of *USA Weekend*, in an interview with Terry McMillan, author of *Waiting to Exhale*, she was asked, "What is the biggest challenge for women today?" To which she replied, "Maintaining integrity and juggling family, career and love life" (McMillan, 1995). The message seems to be that no matter what professional or personal avenue you may choose in life, maintaining your integrity is and should always be of paramount concern. Assuring ourselves of continual growth in all aspects of our lives seems to be indelibly possible as long as we believe in ourselves. Often, it takes an unexpected juncture in life that jars us into the awareness of our own strength. Freda experienced this while on her own with three small children and working to complete her doctoral studies. She states, "I learned again, as I needed to, that I had a lot to contribute, that life still held promise, and I could do anything I set my mind to do."

Belief in self and the things we hold dear will make it possible for us to persevere and maintain our integrity while striving for our goals.

6

Lesson 6: Reach Out to and Through Others

I had joined the California Association of School Business Officials and was an active member of a research and development committee, so I used this network to secure a position prior to the end of the school year, at a significant increase in salary (20%+).

—Catherine

My advice to new women superintendents is to network heavily. The Women's Caucus of the American Association of School Administrators was particularly helpful. It was through them that I met two top-notch, high powered role models. . . . It is also crucial to have a strong support system in place while you are in the job. Daily experiences are so unpredictable; trauma can assail you at any moment.

—Brenda

A major problem for women in the *culture of educational administration* is the obvious lack of adequate networks, positive role models, and support systems in general. There is a scarcity of supportive sponsors and mentors among women in educational administration as well as executive positions across all professions (Benton, 1980; Coursen, 1989; Green, 1982; Johnson, 1991; Mellow, 1988; Rist, 1991; Swiderski, 1988; York et al., 1988). Women have traditionally not benefited from having sponsors and mentors to encourage and support their career advancement. On the other hand, the network

among men—informally referred to as the "good old boy system"—
is strong and, although sometimes viewed pejoratively, is often considered a major vehicle used in selecting job candidates (Benton,
1980; Schmuck, 1986). Many successful women executives indicate
the importance of being accepted into or at least being recognized by
the male network because it is the dominant power group in the
profession.

Ironically, female administrators frequently report more reluctant acceptance from the female staff members than from male members. Traditionally oriented women often harbor resentment for and
even openly defy women who break with tradition and assume
positions usually occupied by males (Woo, 1985). Our questionnaire
asked respondents to react to the statement, *Women are supportive of
other women in the profession.* Seventy-three percent of the 150 women
administrators either agreed or strongly agreed with the statement;
the remaining 27% of the respondents were undecided or disagreed
with the statement. Thus, more than one fourth of our national
sampling of women administrators in education do not feel positive
about women's support of other women in the profession. This
finding is supported by other research (e.g., Brown & Merchant, 1993)
and is frequently an issue in the stories of the women in Phase II of
our study. For example, Emily recalls female reactions to her as a new,
young, and first female principal of a high school on the West Coast:

> I expected some of the faculty women to like me, and, maybe
> even enjoy having a woman in leadership. (Remember, this
> was the mid-seventies.) What a shock it was to find no
> loyalty and little support. The counselors and the assistant
> principal were terrific but many of the teachers were, it
> seemed, not inclined to accept leadership from a woman.
> And the women teachers were less inclined!

The prevalence of this attitude is further complicated by some men's
and women's refusal even to acknowledge that problems exist for
women as a gender in their ascent to top-level positions (Biklen &
Brannigan, 1980; Haskell, 1991). Brenda poignantly writes of her own
process of denial, which many women experience:

> I never wanted to believe I had less opportunity than the
> men. I never wanted to believe the cards were stacked

against me. I never wanted to believe that when push comes to shove, people can be mean, base, and self-serving. I never wanted to believe people would almost kill to maintain power and control independent of right or wrong. But those were childish and unrealistic principles.

Top-level female administrators (from which our study's sample was taken) represent fewer than 15% of the administrative workforce in education; they are in key positions to encourage and nurture the leadership potential of promising, aspiring administrators of both genders—especially females who have so few women role models and mentors from whom to find support and guidance. When asked if they were currently a part of a strong network of supportive women in the profession, 40% of the survey respondents said yes; 17% said no and did not see a need to be; 40% said no but would like to be. The fact that the majority of education's top female executives surveyed in this study indicated that they were not part of a strong network of professional support is disturbing; however, for 17% of these women to indicate that they did not even see a *need* for a support system is far more perplexing. Brown and Merchant (1993) address this issue in their research on support systems for women in leadership:

> Women must recognize who they are, accept that they are leaders and role models for those who follow, and gain the self-confidence to convince others. By challenging the barriers they face, by developing networks with all those with whom they come in contact, by choosing and becoming mentors, and by following the advice of those who are now in leadership positions, women can have the support system required to open new doors and to be the "best leader" any position demands. Because many women in education are not aware of the power and importance of [role models and mentors], new thinking may be required. (p. 91)

Our research supports Merchant and Brown's conclusion that many—although clearly not the majority of—women educators remain unaware of, or deny the need for, better support systems for women in the profession. When asked to rank order five reasons frequently given for the underrepresentation of women in administration, *insuf-*

ficient role-modeling, networking, and mentoring among women ranked second, just barely below *cultural stereotyping of "appropriate roles" for men and women.* More than 70% of the women in the study ranked *insufficient support systems* as either the first or second cause for the continued underrepresentation of women in educational administration; fewer than 12% ranked this cause lowest—number 4 or 5 in their priority ranking. Overall, this cause was ranked 1, 2, or 3 more often (89%) than any of the others, including the number-one-ranked cause, *cultural stereotyping* (87%). So, it seems that even among the 17% of respondents who indicated in an earlier question that a support system was not important for *them,* most recognized its overall importance to women's career development in educational administration.

In a separate section of the questionnaire related to career barriers, survey respondents were asked to comment on gender-related barriers they had personally encountered in their career paths. Many of these women administrators responded similarly; the following quotes are representative of their comments about the lack or inadequacy of professional networks and support systems:

> Competing with coaches who were moved ahead and the "good ole boy" system

> University counselors were not supportive of non-traditional female roles in the 60's

> Difficult to break into the "network"

> Scarcity of role models

> Unsupportive, uncooperative women

> Age and gender were factors in my not finding a superintendency . . . AND my not building a network of administrators.

> All the college instructors in school administration were male; they strongly recommended I take another career path.

Another open-ended question in the survey asked respondents to give their best advice to other administrator hopefuls; much of this advice related to developing and maintaining professional and personal support systems. Some of the more typical comments were as follows:

Know the power bases in the organization and the community.

Get the right people to know you and for the right reasons.

Become involved in the community.

Be a nurturer and supporter of others.

Select systems that have a history of mentoring women for positions of power.

Personal Support Systems

Balancing family and career is still a major concern for career women. The women in our study frequently stated that support for their efforts was needed not only in the professional arena but also in their personal lives. These women were sensitive to the fact that their desires to advance professionally were out of the ordinary in traditional terms, and that an integral part of their success was support from their families or other close, personal relationships. A few exemplary comments on this theme include the following:

Marry someone who can handle your success!

Maintain strong, supportive personal relationships and support systems—marriage, family are absolutely essential.

Tend to your personal relationships as astutely as you do your professional ones.

Network, not just for job advancement, but also to learn, to share, and to maintain professional friends.

Many of the women in our study told candidly of the problems they encountered trying to balance personal and professional concerns—particularly dealing with the identity conflicts and role expectations they encountered as wives, mothers, and career women. Chapter 2 deals with many of these problems in the section on barriers created by the demands of both family and career responsibilities.

Throughout the survey, the strong majority of these women administrators reinforced the professional literature's assertion that support systems can play a significant role in career advancement. The importance of having a network of professional and personal acquaintances was often repeated by the respondents. The most surprising finding to the researchers was not that the majority of these top-level administrators had been mentored, were positively supported both personally and professionally, or either were or wanted to be a part of a support group for women. The most surprising result was that at least one fifth of these highly educated women with all of their successes and experiences indicated that they saw no need to be part of a support group of women. Perhaps these women interpreted the survey's statement to be exclusive of men, and they saw no need to be in a network of *women only*. Throughout the survey, many of the women mentioned the need to find support from *both* genders and to be supportive of *both* men and women in the profession. Although the statement was not meant to imply that women were to exclude men from their networks—only that women must make more deliberate attempts to reach out to and through other women for mutual support—perhaps some of the respondents interpreted it that way. No doubt, the notion of being a part of a single-gender support group would have been offensive to some of the respondents who were opposed to either "good old boy" or "good old girl" systems of exclusivity—a sentiment we share.

The stories from our select group of 15 successful women administrators were replete with testimonials of their commitment to reach out to others—both men and women—to give support and help others for the benefit and welfare of an improved profession. Delores's story includes the following example of what many expressed in similar ways:

> Education is under a great deal of challenge and it is vital that we be active in our local civic organizations to help others understand the current needs of education so we will be able to be prepared for the future. I have invested a great deal of my time and energy over my career in helping make

the community I live in one of the best communities, and I will continue to dedicate myself to that goal. Some areas I would stress for those who may read this account is the importance of friends and family. They have provided a solid base to build my career and my life on, and I count on them every day of my life. I try to give back to them a portion of what they have given to me and that is an invaluable source of strength to me. . . . I want to help attract the best and the brightest to the field and will do all that I can through my work with the [state withheld] Association of School Administrators and the American Association of School Administrators who offer scholarships for those interested in pursuing a career in education. I currently serve as the chair of the scholarship committee for [the state] and have served in this role for six years. I will dedicate myself to that task as long as I am allowed to continue in the role, since it gives me one very promising way to assist other educators.

According to more than 70% of these randomly sampled, female executives' responses as well as a growing body of research reported in the literature, women's career advancement in the field of educational administration can be significantly enhanced by improved support systems. Based on this study, the stories, and the literature, recommendations to career women for developing and maintaining support systems include the following:

1. Strategically build networks of support—both personally and professionally, formally and informally.
2. Join professional organizations that support gender-fair practices.
3. Be actively, intentionally supportive of (and certainly not *hostile* toward) other women who choose administrative careers.
4. Apply in school districts with a history of fair employment and promotion practices.
5. Become politically active and involved in civic affairs.
6. When in a position to make organizational and cultural changes, work hard to improve the system for the adults as well as the children by encouraging gender-fair policy and practice in the workplace.

The success story of Sarah is excerpted below to illustrate her keen regard for and skill in professional networking for mutual support, her political awareness, and her loyalty and devotion to maintaining strong family ties. Sarah is currently a district superintendent of schools in the western part of the nation. She is also a wife and mother of six children. She is of Spanish descent and has pioneered several executive positions in education with her gender and racial combination.

Sarah's Story

The most appropriate time and place for me to start my career path is in a small farming community during World War II, during my early teens. During World War II there was no gender bias because, in essence, women had no male competitors. In the schools, there were many female principals and county superintendents. Many schools in the state had not been consolidated into districts at this time. County superintendents were elected during regular elections. Teaching was a very attractive profession, especially if you were brought up in a rural setting. I always thought teachers were well-to-do because they owned cars and had cameras!

My parents were farmers who made their living from the land and a few cattle. In 1942, all of my brothers were drafted into the armed services. No male was left to help my father with the farming chores. I inherited the farming jobs that my brothers had left behind. I think of this period of my life as the turning point because of the attitude that had developed toward the working woman. They were viewed as capable of taking over male jobs. This developed a sense of liberation.

The World War II era was a very enlightening period. The war effort unified families and neighbors, and the nation as a whole worked together. Women were the only ones left behind to put together planes, tanks, and other equipment. It was a period of renaissance for women. We grew as individuals and gained the feeling of equality. After the war was over, it was back to square one! The men came home, they took over the jobs, and women went back to the kitchen (for the most part, anyway)!

It seems necessary to give this background because I need to explain why I never felt subservient to any male, since I was a young girl. I felt I could do just about any male task as well as or better than they could. I became confident.

My formal schooling took place in _____ County during my elementary grades. I attended junior and senior high school in a western state. After graduating from high school, I attended college. I worked my way through school, so I would take a year off to teach. There was a shortage of teachers in the state at that time, and persons with some college credits were granted temporary teaching certificates.

In 1955, my husband and I were married during Thanksgiving break. He was working at the VA Hospital and I was teaching at an elementary school. After I finished my contract, we decided to move to another city and get our degrees.

I got a teaching job in a school district close to the university. I received my BS degree in 1957. The district had a policy which did not allow a teacher to teach if she was more than four months pregnant. I went to the superintendent to let him know that I was pregnant and that I would have to resign because of this policy. He knew I needed the job in order for my husband to continue school and in order for me to be covered under my insurance. I was beyond myself when he said, "Well, pregnant women have to eat too. We will ignore it for the time being."

In 1958, when my husband graduated, I quit my teaching job to raise my family. At this time, we moved to another location to make our home. My husband had gotten a job there as a medical lab technician in the local hospital.

I stayed home until 1965, longer than I had expected. But in the interim, there were more children, six in all. I remember mentioning to my friends about my intentions to return to work. Some of the comments were not too flattering. One of them asked, "You are going to neglect your children to go to work?" to which I responded, "It's not the quantity of mothering that is important, but rather the quality that counts."

I never felt guilty, for two reasons: I felt that I had learned good parenting skills from my parents, plus from all the training I had received in child psychology. I also wanted to help my husband provide, so that our children would be able to attend college. My parents were very excited about my returning to the classroom. They felt I was putting to use what I had gone to college for, instead of "wasting" my education. I never felt I wasted anything. I have fantastic memories of my children's childhoods and the things we did together. They also recount the fun they had when growing up.

Upon returning to the classroom, I immediately had my eye on a principalship. I felt this was the place where the action was. I knew that in order for me to gain this position, I had to first have my credentials, with the proper degree and certification. This was not hard for me to accomplish. What I felt I also needed to do was to be visible—extra-ordinary in the classroom and active in the community. [Early on, Sarah realized the importance of "reaching out" into the community. She always considers her support system as she progesses with her story.]

I was a very cooperative employee. I offered my services wherever I was needed. I became very active in teachers' organizations, locally and statewide. I did, in fact, become very visible. I was often called to speak as an officer of the National Education Association and was often interviewed by the local newspaper. I established great rapport with parents and school patrons. This was very important, because later on in my career, I used this influence to achieve some of my goals.

I had been in the classroom in the local schools for twelve years and was working on my master's degree, when I was offered a head teacher's job in an outlying school. I don't think anyone applied for this position. It was not a very attractive one, because the expectation was that whoever took over the position had to convince the parents that the best thing for students in this school was to close it. It had to be done smoothly and with minimal controversy.

I took the teaching principal job. I concentrated all year on convincing the parents and community that the best thing for the students was to be transported to a nearby school in the city. The selling points were the courses offered and the exposure to a more worldly environment. Also, because they would eventually be transported to the junior high school, this would make it an easier transition. The school was closed as smoothly as possible.

During the summer of 1973, I received my master's degree. Now I was armed with the proper credentials. A principal's position opened and I applied for it. The opening was at the school where students from the closed school were to attend. What followed was a revelation to me.

The superintendent and the board received a barrage of calls from parents and patrons requesting that I be appointed as principal, so that the students and staff who were being transferred would have a familiar face as their leader. I was appointed as principal. It was at this point that I became aware that administrative positions were somewhat political. [Note how Sarah makes use of this important awareness!] I probably would have gotten the position anyway, but boards are known to bend to the pressure of their constituency.

On the board were two of my classmates from high school. It had never occurred to me to contact them for help in getting me the position. They were hurt because I had not done so. Everyone assumed that I had political power because of these two board members. I pretended that I did and used it to the hilt!

I served as elementary school principal in the same school for four years. It was one of the most satisfying periods of my career. It seemed as if that was where the action was for someone who wanted to make a difference in the delivery of service for elementary students. It was where the action was, but not for long. It seems that we, in the central office, sometimes tend to stifle the enthusiasm of persons who are in direct control of the teaching act and methods. At least that's what I perceived at the time.

There was another female elementary principal in the district. However, she retired after I had been there a year. I was the only female left in the whole administrative group. There were seven principals in the district: one high school, one junior high and five elementary. We formed a small organization in order to influence policy and to initiate changes we felt were needed. I was usually the spokesperson of the group when we met with central office personnel.

I attended every board meeting, so that we knew exactly what was going on. I enjoyed this very much because it gave me visibility and I learned how board meetings were conducted. I was able to analyze the power structure—when to speak or when to ask questions, as well as when to keep my mouth shut. [Understanding politics, how to work with people, is an obvious plus in Sarah's career.]

Through our group, we were able to initiate a lot of changes we wanted. We also were able to negotiate a salary schedule that reflected our training and our experience, such as the one the teachers had. Later on, we just went with the teachers' schedule and were paid for additional times as per schedule, plus a very nice increment for the different principalships.

In 1975, the superintendent resigned. The search for a new superintendent started and I applied, not so much because I thought I had a chance of getting it, but rather to let the board and the community know that I was interested. [Another example of her understanding the importance of visibility and being known in the community.] To my surprise, I was one of three finalists. The director of instruction was named superintendent and I made sure I was the first one to congratulate him and offer my help wherever he needed me.

In the meantime, the composition of the board changed. The superintendent was relieved of his duties at the end of his contract. Actually, I knew before he did. One of the board members came to me to tell me, in the strictest of confidence, what was going to occur at the board meeting on June 14, 1977. She came to me and wanted me to swear that I would not repeat what she was about to reveal. I agreed. What followed shocked me.

She asked me if I was ready for the superintendency. I said I had been for the last two years. She said that she had been sent by her fellow board members to tell me that if I wanted it, I could have it, but under certain conditions. I asked her what the conditions were. The plan was to not renew his contract and immediately someone would move to name me the next superintendent. I jumped in and said "Without advertising it?" She said yes. She reminded me how conservative our community was and how they might not take to a female heading the largest employer in the community. I was rather stunned, and at first I felt cheated that I would not have the privilege of competing against other applicants. After I thought it over (for two seconds!), I thought, "Take it while the offer is still good." So I told her that I would be more than happy to accommodate them!

The night of the board meeting when this took place, I understand that the crowd was in shock. The executive, closed session lasted for hours and the audience was wondering what was going on. I was at my home, waiting for the call to tell me that I had been appointed. It was twelve o'clock and no call. Then, finally, at 1:30 in the morning, the business manager called to give me the news that I was the next superintendent.

The following day, the telephone did not stop ringing. Calls came from the staff, the town's people and from all over the state. It had not even entered my mind that I would be making history. I found out that I was the first female to be appointed as district superintendent in my state. So, the newspaper and television interviews followed.

Later on, I found out that not only was I the first female superintendent in the state, but was also the first Hispanic female superintendent to be appointed to a district in the nation. I want to emphasize *appointed* because there were several elected superintendents. This news initiated several calls from all over the United States and locally. The media also started calling for interviews. Overnight, I became a novelty. Because of this, I was in demand for speaking engagements.

Let me tell you about the experiences I encountered as a female superintendent. On July 1st, my first day in the office, I remember that all the females were very happy to see me here. I don't think the males were too keen on seeing their buddy out of his office. It was customary for all central office staff members to take their coffee break at 10:00 a.m. That first day, I did not know where to sit, because I did not want to make any waves. The business manager pointed to a chair and said, "This chair is yours. The girls have been warming it up for you." I said, "Thank you girls, and who warmed it up for you, Josh?" There was complete silence.

Shortly after, I wanted the business manager to brief me on the budget, although I was already pretty familiar with it. During our meeting he said to me, "Sarah, I ask only one thing of you. This is a pretty rough job and things aren't always pleasant. When things get tough, please don't cry." I was a little peeved, and answered, "I promise you I won't cry, but you have to promise me you won't cry either." This didn't go over very well, but it stopped the innuendos for a while.

The superintendent from the neighboring school district was going from contracted buses to school owned buses. He wanted to borrow two or three buses from our district until his came in. He completely ignored me as the superintendent and borrowed the buses from the director of transportation. When I found out about the buses, I told the director, "I sure hope they don't have an accident, because I didn't authorize this move. Furthermore, I haven't even told the board about it. They are not going to be very happy."

My first month as a superintendent was very interesting and a lot of fun. We were in the process of re-roofing the junior high school. When the contractor finally started, I went to see the project. Both the maintenance director and the business manager didn't want me to climb the roof to check on the materials and progress of the job. I said, "Don't worry. I've been on top of a building before." Oh yes, I was wearing a pant suit!

As I said before, I was in demand for speaking engagements. During one of these engagements, I was asked how could I be both superintendent and a mother of six children. I answered with a quote I had read somewhere: "God gave me a good brain and a good uterus, and I have used them both!" This ended the sexist questions and comments. The discussion moved to more relevant material.

Ours was a very unique district. It was known for promoting from within. There were three ex-superintendents working under me in the district. The business manager was one of them, one was an elementary principal, and one was the high school principal. This was hard because I always felt that they were just waiting for me to make a boo-boo. This made me work harder and better. I have always performed better under pressure anyway.

Although the business manager might have been a pain, he also was the most helpful. He was known for his expertise in the budgeting process and was known throughout the state. He also introduced me to key people at the state department. I learned the lobbying process from him. He was good at it and was well respected by the local legislators.

A superintendent's meeting was held out of town during this first month. I, of course, was the only female there. I was welcomed. I never felt out of place, except during the social part of the gathering. My husband was unable to go with me, so I found myself looking for entertainment outside the group. I was sitting in the lobby of the hotel, when the superintendent from the neighboring school district (the one who had borrowed the buses) showed up and asked me what I was doing sitting in the lobby. I told him that I was waiting for a shuttle to go to the horse races. I revealed my vice and he said, "Do you play poker?" I said yes. He invited me to join other superintendents who usually played poker after these meetings. I said, "Sure! Do you think they would mind?" He said, "Why should they? You are one of us."

This was the beginning of a most beautiful relationship that I enjoyed with my colleagues. The poker games were always announced during the meetings as the "probability seminars." We knew what this meant. The poker playing group included the assistant state superintendent, who later became (and still is) the state superintendent. You have no idea how many deals were transacted between districts and between the state department and districts. It was so educational for me. I learned who had clout and how to approach them. I learned where to go and who to talk to when I needed something for my district. The director of school finance also belonged to this group. And needless to say, our budget hearings went so well that our board was stunned that we didn't have to make changes.

During that first year, a suit was won by parents of mentally handicapped children from my state which demanded that the state's public schools participate in 194-142 law to procure funds for special education programs and to provide equal educational services for handicapped children. All public schools were mandated to serve these students. In a nearby (10 miles) town, there is a state institution, a hospital and training school, where many mentally and physically handicapped people had been served. The school district in that town was getting a lot of flack from parents and patrons who did not want regular students to be exposed to the behavior of the mentally handicapped children.

The State Department of Education did not wish to waste time in litigation, because they had to serve this group of students. They wanted to expedite the move, so they came to our district for help. They asked us if we would serve these students in our district. We, of course, agreed, provided that we were furnished with handicapped-equipped buses, a building with proper furniture, and equipment and funding for additional staff. The department was more than happy to accommodate us. We received everything we requested. Our district became the model for the rest of the state. Our facility was a state-of-the-art structure at the time. Personnel from other districts came to visit and get ideas on what was needed to house special education students, especially the more severe cases. The state department became forever indebted to us because this eliminated litigation and saved the department millions of dollars. From then on, my clout was immeasurable. I collected on that favor forever!

Sometimes all of this information does not sound relevant to my career path. I guess what I am trying to establish is how one becomes known and visible in administrative circles. This also makes your tenure somewhat more stable and secured.

When reading this, one might think, "When did she have time to run the district?" In a middle-sized district, which my district is, you have assistant central office administrators who tend to the daily operation of the schools. These administrators include the business manager and curriculum directors for both the elementary and secondary levels. You have access to maintenance and transportation directors and also a person who is in charge of all matters which relate to the staff. These people would brief me on everything that was going on in the district and what needed to be done; Monday mornings were dedicated to these briefings. I either gave them direction or approved what they suggested. Principals were included in these sessions also. From the principals, we were brought up to date on progress of classroom information and their needs from each department.

The superintendent's job in a district such as this is more as a public relations person. Your task is to keep the board informed on almost every area pertaining to the delivery of all services. The superintendent also keeps the community informed of how, when, and where services to students are delivered. One's time is consumed with speaking to groups within the community. Parents are kept informed through the principals. The news media is also used almost daily to impart pertinent information. The superintendent must also represent the district at different social functions, such as funerals, weddings and so on. It is also very important for the superintendent to be part of the town's chamber of commerce. The schools are considered as one of the local businesses, especially if the district is the largest employer. Your working day is not normal. It continues into the night. You are on call 24 hours a day. You have to attend many school functions, such as games, concerts, PTA meetings, and one has to make sure you have not omitted anyone. [Do you see why we chose Sarah to demonstrate "reaching out to and through people"?]

What about one's home and personal life? Sacrifices are costly. We are a large family unit. When major changes were to occur, especially if it interrupted our regular routine, we had discussions with our children. We always pointed out the benefits as well as the consequences of the decision to follow a different course. When I took the principalship, our children knew of the additional time I would spend away from home. Chores were assigned to each, with rewards at the end of the school year, such as a nice family vacation to spots where we would otherwise not be able to afford. Our children were always very helpful, so this arrangement was no problem. My husband was also very accommodating. He always encouraged me to achieve and work toward my goals. I think that his having to help with the cooking and other house chores during his college work while I provided really helped.

As superintendent, my time was even more in demand. I was never home before six in the evening. There were also several out-of-town and overnight trips. By this time our two older sons were gone to college, so there was less laundry, less cooking, and one less room to clean. I also had a live-in relative who needed employment and a place to live, which helped immensely. Before I took the job as superintendent, I made sure my husband was aware that I would be traveling out of town and overnight with mostly men. Most of the meetings were with men, but this never bothered him. What was rather uncomfortable to him was the scheduled entertainment for spouses that were arranged. These functions were geared toward the spouse who was the homemaker. What he really enjoyed were the national and regional conventions, because he would schedule tours on his own.

In 1981—I think I have the right year—I was invited by the American Association of School Administrators and by the Director of Minority Affairs with this prestigious organization, to speak at a Women's Caucus. There were approximately 75 top school administrators from throughout the United States. The panel was made up of female superintendents from different parts of the United States. We talked about the problems we encountered as females in an area that was dominated by males. We talked about how men form the buddy system among themselves and how they stand together to help their buddies move into administrative positions.

Out of this gathering evolved a very prolific group of women who were to go out and promote other women into administrative positions. The director of minority affairs had acquired a grant to organize a group called "Aware West" which started training seminars in a couple of states for aspiring women who were interested in administrative positions in their districts or elsewhere. At these seminars, we taught them how to organize their resumes, had simulated interviews, and suggested how to dress, sit, and carry themselves.

After this first gathering, the women superintendents started having regular meetings prior to the national convention of the AASA. Other female school administrators started attending these meetings. At the end of these meetings, we had a reception where several big-shot headhunters were invited. Ironically, all the headhunters were men. They were hired to do superintendent searches by school districts from everywhere and this was quite an attraction for those women who were ready to move on to superintendent positions. This phase of my career was one of the most rewarding for me. I came in contact with so many influential educators from throughout the United States. The friendship that developed between the director and myself was, and still is, one of those rare privileges that has come my way.

After working with "Aware West," we wanted to expand this training for women in my state, so with the director's help, we organized an "Aware" group. By this time in my state, we had welcomed another female superintendent. She too became very active in the network. The following year, the largest district in my city named its first female superintendent, a woman who had been a district superintendent in one of the "Aware West" states. I had met her at the AASA meetings before she came to our state.

Through my association with the director of minority affairs, I was recognized by the association and named to several committees. My out-of-state travel was increasing. I also became a proposal reader for the Office of Education. My mentor in the school board was becoming a little uncomfortable with this situation, so I started to turn speaking requests down. She felt I was more interested in promoting myself than our schools. The other board members felt I was good publicity for our district. I had a conflict within myself, because I felt I owed my mentor my loyalty. The tension was getting thick.

In 1984, a new governor was elected. A very close friend of mine was his campaign manager. She was named as his top administrative assistant and she became a very powerful figure during the governor's tenure. At that time, the public school finance office was under the governor. The executive secretary of the state schools' Finance Office had tremendous power throughout the state. This was the most coveted position in our state's educators' circle.

Through my friend's influence, I was able to dole out political favors, even to the department of education. For my school district, I was able to acquire over six million dollars for building projects. My friend would also call to find out who merited funding for requests that he may have not been familiar with. My friend was also known as the main gate-keeper to the governor's office. If someone needed access to the governor and could not get in, they would call on me to see if my friend would help them.

Through this association, I also received a tremendous honor. I was named as regent at one of the state's universities, a position I held for six years. This was a most rewarding experience for me. I learned the working of both sides of the table.

I had been the district's superintendent for eight years. The composition of the board changed in February of 1985. Two or three years back, there had been a football coaching position opening. A junior high school physical education teacher wanted this assignment, but did not get it. After that meeting, which had to be moved to the junior high gymnasium, this particular teacher warned me, saying "You are going to regret this action, you and the athletic director." I ignored it, not realizing what he meant.

As I mentioned before, in 1985 the composition of the board changed. The physical education teacher ran for the board and won. Lo and behold, everything went berserk. The entire board was in turmoil. They disagreed among themselves, and it became split. Unfortunately, two were in my favor, three against. My contract was not up for renewal until 1986. I had already informed the board that I was going to retire at the end of my contract. The board was made up of my mentor, three other previous board members, and the new member who had a vendetta to satisfy.

The new board member came to me to tell me that he and two other board members wanted me to fire five administrators in my staff. I said no. Two or three days later, he came back with a list of names—the three he wanted out. He put the list on my desk. I picked it up and threw it in the trash. He said that if I did not comply with their request, I was going to be fired. I said "So be it!" When he left my office, I picked up the list he had given me. The following day, I went to a lawyer with the list and recounted all that was taking place. He told me we would not do anything until I was actually fired. The following board meeting, I was put on administrative leave with pay. One of the elementary principals was named as interim superintendent. It was a month before they decided to fire me, listing several reasons, none of them true as it was proven at a hearing later on. In the meantime, my mentor came to offer me the business manager's job. I told her she was offering me a position that was already filled. She said, "Not for long."

This, by the majority of the board, threw the community in an uproar. A group tried to impeach the three board members, but they were so shrewd and had people with the committee who actually had not followed the recalling process to the letter. I found this out from some very reliable sources later on. This was a very chaotic time for the community. To this date, there is a feeling of division. Needless to say, it was traumatic for my family and myself. One of the things about a personal tragedy is that when you have not done anything wrong, it doesn't bother you as much. I did not worry about it, but it was very hard on my family.

When I was finally fired, I requested an open hearing much to their chagrin. They thought I was going to ask for a closed hearing. I wanted everyone who was curious to attend, so that the town's people would know I was clean. The hearing was held at the high school auditorium from two o'clock in the afternoon until midnight. The auditorium was packed with news media, television, and cameras. I do not want to bore you with the details of the hearing. I do, however, want to talk about one line of questioning that was hilarious. Remember the list of administrators that the new board member gave me? My attorney brought it out and asked the board member, "Is this your writing?" "Yes." "Did you give it to Sarah?" "No." "How did she get it?" "I don't know." "You gave it to her. This, ladies and gentlemen, is Mr. X's 'Hit List.'"

A week later, my attorney called me and told me that they were willing to buy my contract as a settlement. I took it and cried all the way to the bank! I retired and remained retired for four years—not totally. I was doing a lot of consulting work, mostly out of state. I took a job with the county as director of several senior citizen centers. I did this for two years. In all, I was away from direct school business for six years. My plan and dream had always been to be superintendent in a small district, because I always felt that in my state, young, climbing educators took the superintendent's position in small districts just to learn the business and then move to bigger districts where salary was more attractive.

In May, 1991, I was reading the want ads in the local newspaper under education. I always have done so, because I like to keep up to see who of my former colleagues were retiring. I came across the advertisement for a superintendent's job in a city in my state. It caught my eye and I decided I'd take a stab at it. I told my husband about it and he said, "Why not? Go for it!" I did, wanting it but not expecting it. I got my papers in order, just like we had trained all the young women to do.

I was in Washington, DC, reading proposals for the office of education, when my husband called and told me to return a call to a board member in the city where I had applied. An interview was scheduled and here I am at it again. I thought I would probably be here one or two years at the most, but I am going on my fourth!

The city I'm in now is a rural community in the southwest part of the state. The population consists of about 500 people. It is in the largest county in the state, but as advertised, "It has more elk than people." The main industry here is ranching and logging—the latter has almost disappeared, thanks to the spotted owl.

I have to mention how I might have been preferred over other applicants that applied for this job. [Another example of how her familiarity with important people in the profession paid off.] The superintendent, who was here prior to my coming here, was doing the search for the board. I had known him through my work in administrative associations throughout the state. I am told by the people who are still here that when he saw my application he said, "This is it. This is the person who I would like to leave in my place. You would be left in good hands with this lady." There were two finalists: a former local high school principal and myself. The former superintendent recommended me, and I was voted in. History repeating itself, I was the first female and the first Hispanic to serve as superintendent here.

It has been so much fun to run a school district again. When I started attending educational state meetings, it was a big surprise to many of my former colleagues that I came back. I refer to myself sometimes as the "recycled superintendent." I have not found it too hard to regain some of the clout I used to have, because there are still a lot of familiar faces in the state Department of Education. For one, the state superintendent is the same person who was there when I left the system.

Last year, my business manager and I were begging for an increase in funding to give decent teacher raises. I got tired of begging and I told my business manager, "What are we doing here, talking to the angels, when we can be talking to God?" We went directly to the state superintendent to get what we wanted. I don't know if this impressed her, but you could see the look on her face, like "Are you serious?"

This is a very small district and the tasks are so different from where I had been before. You sort of have to become a "jack of all trades." The local school board is so great to work for. The only drawback in this district is that it is such a poor district financially. It has become a very depressed area because what was once a rich area for logging, the controversial spotted owl has curtailed these people's livelihood. The logging industry is gone and with it went the sawmill. People have had to move away to provide for their families and it has hurt the schools by a loss of enrollment. Bond issues and mill levies are hard to pass, so we don't have money to adequately maintain our facilities. Fortunately for the schools, I know where to go to acquire some funds to help out with needed improvements. This is what I mean when I say new and inexperienced superintendents cheat districts such as this one. They just come and go without doing the district justice. Seasoned superintendents know where to go for help, and that is just what I have managed to do.

When I came for an interview, I knew this was a remote and isolated area. I knew I could handle it because I had been brought up on a farm. I had forgotten that our farm was only fifteen miles from town, not three hours. So the staff had a good time with my trying to adjust to the lack of city services. During my first week, I asked the people in the office if everyone sold wood, because every household seemed to have at least five cords stacked up. They said no—that was about a year's supply. So this meant I better plan on using the wood stove and ordering some wood. I then asked when was the trash picked up and they informed me that it was picked up any time I wanted, because all I had to do was pick it up and take it to the dump. I did get even with them though. One day, one of the office girls went outside and came back all shook up about a traffic jam in front of the elementary school. I went to look for myself. I did not want an accident to occur. There were five cars. I came in with a grin on my face and asked, "Five cars is a traffic jam?" She said, "In this city it is."

There isn't much I can add to the superintendency as far as the daily operation of the schools. One thing that is very satisfying, people are very humble and they appreciate anything one does to improve the delivery of services. Politics, just like any district in the state, plays an important part in the administrative game. At this stage of my career though, it is easier to handle because you can always come back and say, "Hey, I don't need this hassle. I don't have to work." This works wonders in trying to maintain a professional attitude in doing what is best for the district and to keep the board happy and out of trouble.

This concludes my career path, but I want to prove to you that in achieving the highest post in a public school, I have not neglected my family, nor have I developed ulcers over incidents that have been adverse along the way. In positions just as this, you have to expect good times and bad times. That goes with the territory. It has been an excellent career, both psychologically and financially. Everyone should try to reach that last step. I am planning to retire at the end of my contract, June 30, 1995.

I also want to mention that along the way, I have promoted women to administrative positions, one of them to the principalship and one as director of transportation. This is not a large number because they were the only ones who showed interest.

As I said, I did not neglect my family. Here is a synopsis of who they are and what they are doing. Our oldest son is an attorney. He has two daughters and has full custody of both. Our second son is single and is also an attorney in our state. Our oldest daughter is married, has two children and is a school teacher, but has taken a leave from the classroom to raise her children. Our next daughter is married, has one child and is an elementary school teacher in a local school district. We also have a son who is a beautiful young man with Down Syndrome and is being taken care of by my husband. Our youngest daughter is single and enjoying her work as an associate manager with the Wal-Mart stores. She travels all over the continental United States, Mexico, and Canada setting up new stores and training new employees. My husband is retired, which allows me to be more mobile. He also takes care of our handicapped son. We always laugh about this because we agree that I took care of him for 30 years, now it's his turn. We say this because his job was even more demanding than mine. He was on call 24 hours a day and he was not able to spend as much time with our children as I did.

7

Lesson 7: Practice What You Seek: The Importance of Mentoring

> The bottom line to mentoring, I think, is to care enough about the individual to share and to provide information to all those who could possibly need it. I find no good reason for withholding information from anyone just to increase the dependency of people on others. Information is power. Everyone ought to have it.
>
> —*Elizabeth*

Closely allied with networking as an important part of building support systems for women aspiring to and those in positions of administration is *mentoring*. The more recent literature (e.g., Garland, 1991; Lynch, 1990; Myers, 1992; Pavan, 1987), as well as our research results, focuses on the importance of women having mentors—either male or female—in order to make significant advances in administrative careers. Of course, the flip side of this issue is the need for women to *be* mentors to others, especially to women who typically have so few female mentors from whom to draw support.

An obvious part of the problem with women's lack of a support system is due to the low numbers of females in executive positions in education as well as the even fewer number of female professors of educational administration (fewer than 2%). Women professors and female executives have an important role to play as positive models and mentors for other women. They also serve as important contributors to the image of women as leaders for both school districts and the public-at-large (Short et al., 1989). With so few females available to mentor their junior colleagues, many women have relied on males to be their sponsors. For some, like Delores, this has worked well. Delores's career story frequently includes references to many of her mentors. She always speaks positively about her mentors—most of whom were male—and about her commitment to give to others the kind of support and mentoring she received:

> I find it somewhat troubling to realize that women were not available in my early career years to serve as mentors for me or others to become administrators. I was one of the fortunate ones to have great male role models and mentors to encourage and nurture me as I began my career. As I indicated in my earlier statements, I was indeed happy to find two great women mentors during my years in Delta Kappa Gamma, who held out great hope and challenge for me and encouraged me every step of the way, not only in words, but in actions and by directing me to scholarships which greatly assisted me at that time. I am forever indebted to my great mentors and hope that I may give back to other educators and assist them as I have been so ably assisted.

Overall, women have had difficulty developing the alliances they need because older male executives and male professors typically prefer protégées who are junior versions of themselves (Garland, 1991). As Biklen and Brannigan (1980) have noted:

> Since women who have entered male fields are often seen as outsiders, they lack acceptance by those in the mainstream and are often perceived as strange or different. Because they are outsiders they rarely have equal access to mentors as do their male colleagues in graduate school, they are often not part of the casual network of relationships formed during graduate training, and they may find themselves on the edge rather than in the middle of the professional, socialization process. (p. 15)

Adding insult to injury in the plight of women's support systems is the phenomenon known as the "queen bee" syndrome. This occurs when a woman in a position of authority works to keep other women out to protect her "queenly" status (Benton, 1980). "One of the explanations for this phenomenon," writes Linda Ginn (1989), "has to do with power. Because a large portion of women have been excluded from the power structure of 'out of home' decision-making, they become anxious that there is not enough power to go around" (p. 9). The concept of power shared being power gained seems difficult to grasp for members of minority groups not usually included in the power loop. Unfortunately, this counterproductive attitude also exists among many underrepresented female administrators.

Two of the 14 pages in our original questionnaire were devoted entirely to soliciting information about these women administrators' experiences with and perceptions about their support systems, mentoring, and networking in the profession. One of the questions asked respondents to describe their most significant role models (both positive and negative) and mentors. Information asked about the role model and/or mentor included the model's or mentor's relationship to respondent, gender, age, and chief characteristics. Because so much confusion exists about the meanings of *mentor* and *role model*, these terms were defined by the researchers for this study and were included in the directions to respondents in the questionnaire. A positive role model was defined as "one whom you admired and tried to emulate, but may not have known personally." A *negative role model* was defined as "one whose characteristics or behaviors you have tried to avoid." And a *mentor* was defined as "one with whom you formed a professional, interpersonal relationship and who provided beneficial career and psychosocial support to you." We arrived at these definitions after analysis of a wide array of literature on the topic (e.g., Hennig & Jardim, 1977; Kanter, 1983; Kram, 1983; Levinson, 1978; Phillips, 1978; Welch, 1993).

Of the 151 survey respondents, 85% indicated having had positive role models; 15% left this portion of the questionnaire blank. Seventy-four percent indicated having had negative role models. Seventy-three percent included mentors—many of them reported having had more than one; 27% did not include mentors in their questionnaire responses. These results confirm that the majority of these highly successful women educators have had significant numbers of positive role models and supportive mentors in their lives. Considering the purported scarcity of mentors available to women, this data may suggest that the successful women in educational administration are indeed the more fortunate ones who have had outstanding role models and the support of mentors. This would substantiate the increasing regard for more and better mentors and role models for women reported in the literature. These results also could be interpreted to mean that the availability of role models and mentors for women is now greater than in the past. In either case, these results indicate that women aspiring to educational administration would be wise to look to positive role models and seek mentors to advance their career potential.

The literature on mentor-protégée relationships is not always positive (e.g., Welch, 1993). Some of it warns about the dangers of mixed-gender mentor-protégée relationships becoming sexually intimate or creating rumors of such whether or not well founded; the potential for the relationship to go awry as the protégée grows as a professional equal to or surpassing the mentor; the false security and isolation from a broader network that can result from overreliance on one person, the mentor; or the potential for abusive treatment of the protégée by the mentor. Although the vast majority of the women in our study reported only positive mentoring experiences, one of our storytellers—Harriet—mentioned the problem she experienced with one of her mentoring relationships. She writes, "I had an excellent mentor and as he moved up, he opened doors for me. The problem was that when he left the district, I was no longer in demand."

Despite the potential complications in a mentor-protégée relationship, the respondents in this study reported primarily positive mentoring experiences. When asked to describe the current status of reported mentor relationships, most of them indicated that the relationship was ongoing in a collegial context rather than having ended with the mentor-protégée phase. For example, Delores writes of one of her mentors, "[He] had moved on to become superintendent in another school system, but continued to encourage me as all good mentors do." And, in Elizabeth's description of her current relationship with mentors, she reports:

> I have mentors today generally through a very dynamic support group of other men and women throughout the state who pride themselves on staying on the cutting edge of research and of practice. We meet in a retreat setting twice a year for a long weekend and study, reflect, and dialogue. We are a group of about 30 people, most of whom are assistant

superintendents and staff developers. We are 95 percent female. When we return from these study groups, we feel renewed and energized. We maintain fairly close contact during the periods between these retreats via telephone and fax. We also make it a point to let everyone know about unique training opportunities that are available throughout the state and try to get together during those occasions as well. Whether it is a group like this or a different kind of group or maybe even a single person, I feel strongly that everyone on the firing line must have a support system in order to maintain the perspective that we need to make the right decisions for the students within our schools.

Survey respondents reported a wide variety of people (friends, relatives, colleagues, supervisors, professors, principals, superintendents, and teachers) who had served as positive role models and mentors, with the vast majority of them being school personnel. Many of the role models—both positive and negative—were respondents' former teachers. The majority of mentors were superintendents, principals, or professors. More than two thirds of the respondents reported that their mentors were older than they were and were male. Most of the mentor-protégée relationships were described as superintendent-subordinate, principal-teacher, or professor-student/graduate assistant.

An interesting finding related to negative role models: almost one half of this category were reported to be female—a greater proportion of females than was reported in either of the two more positive categories of role models and mentors. Also interesting was the fact that most of the respondents who reported *positive* role models and mentors also usually included *negative* role models whose behaviors they had tried to avoid. Unfortunately, it seems successful female educational administrators have been motivated to be *different* from almost as much as they have been motivated to be *like* people and administrators they have known—and half of these less than uplifting folks were females! Many of the female negative role models were reported as "dependent" mothers, "paranoid, vicious" bosses, or "insensitive, overbearing" teachers. In the absence of positive female role models and mentors, perhaps women who aspire to male-dominated positions mold professional development and chart career paths by *avoiding* characteristics and behaviors of less than admirable women (as well as some men) whom they are determined *not* to emulate.

That most of these successful women administrators in our study indicated they had experienced negative role models almost as frequently as they had positive role models and mentors was too prevalent to ignore. Motivation to be different or behave differently from someone no doubt can be powerful. From where, then, do one's ideals come? Most likely, positive and negative role models play interactively to motivate one to strive for and against certain behaviors and characteristics. Ultimately, one's ideal model probably is uniquely shaped by the complex combinations of one's positive *and* negative experiences. Because very little was found about negative role models in the literature, additional research may be needed to determine how common this phenomenon is, how it occurs, and how powerful it is when compared with positive role models.

Another part of the questionnaire listed 10 of the most commonly named behaviors of mentors and asked respondents who reported having mentors to indicate the degree to which the mentors had exhibited each of these supportive behaviors. Using a 5-point scale from *almost never* to *almost always*, the respondents rated *communicating* (95%) and *motivating* (93%) as the most frequently (*almost always* or *frequently*) exhibited behaviors followed closely by *validating* (92%) and *role-modeling* (88%). The least frequently (*seldom* or *never*) exhibited mentoring behaviors, according to these women administrators, were *protecting* (25%) and *teaching* (10%). The remaining mentoring characteristics—*guiding, advising and counseling, sponsoring, being subtle and not expecting credit*—were reported with varying degrees of frequency. All of these 10 characteristics were reported by at least half of the respondents as very frequently demonstrated by their mentors. Evidently, mentors provide a number of important nurturing dimensions for the protégée. With such a wide array of supportive behaviors, the aspiring administrator with a strong mentor should indeed have a decided advantage over the administrative aspirant going it alone. Because more than 70% of these successful administrators reported having had career mentors, the importance of mentors to career success is strongly supported by this study.

Women's willingness to be a mentor to others—both men and women—is a critically important aspect of increasing women's support systems (Brown & Merchant, 1993). The questionnaire asked respondents if they had ever been a mentor to someone in the profession. All three groups of respondents—superintendents, assistant superintendents, and high school principals—responded very positively to this question. Eighty percent said they had been a mentor to others. Although this number is high, the need for female role models is too significant to discount the 20% of these top women administrators who have never mentored anyone—male or female. These top-level administrators represent fewer than 15% of the administrative work force in education; they are in key positions to be able to encourage and nurture the leadership potential of promising, aspiring administrators of both genders—especially females who have so few women role models and mentors from whom to find support and guidance.

Again, the most surprising finding related to support systems in this study was not that the majority of these top-level administrators had been mentored, were positively supported both personally and professionally, or either were or wanted to be part of a support group for women. The most unexpected result was that at least one fifth of these highly educated women with all of their successes and experiences indicated that they saw no need to be a part of a support group of women. Perhaps these women saw no need to be in a network of *women only*, and interpreted the wording in the survey to exclude males. Throughout the survey, many of the women mentioned the need to find support from *both* genders and to be supportive of *both* men and women in the profession.

Several of our select 15 women administrators related mentoring experiences as a key part of their career stories. Many of them also reported their experiences as a mentor to others and often expressed a commitment to nurturing leadership potential as a part of their sense of responsibility as a professional educator and leader.

Although it was difficult to select just one that best represented the group, Elizabeth's story was the one we finally chose to exemplify the importance of nurturing and support to career advancement through *mentoring*. From the beginning of Elizabeth's story to the very end, she references the role that mentors played in her career and offers a wealth of advice to women in becoming better mentors. Elizabeth is Assistant Superintendent for Instruction in a school district in the South. She lists insufficient role modeling, networking, and mentoring among women as what she considers to be the number-one reason for women's lack of equitable representation in educational administration, and in the initial survey response, her best advice to other women began with "Find a model." Elizabeth's story follows and clearly demonstrates that she practices what she and a growing number of others preach as desirable behavior for career women.

Elizabeth's Story

The Path to the Top

I began teaching at a middle school with 177 seventh graders in five classes. That was the first year that the school opened and we obviously got many more students than were expected. Since I had done my student teaching in a high school where the university professors sent their children, I was not aware of the strategies that were needed to keep students engaged who did not have enough to eat, who were abused, or who simply did not have the support at home to encourage their education. My first year was definitely a year of learning, talking to other more experienced teachers, and trial and error—mostly error. I had a mentor, though. She was one of the math teachers in the school, and she really took me under her wing. She taught me about the adolescent needs of children, how to encourage them, how to teach them, and how to stand firm when there was a reason to do that. When I was transferred to one of the high schools three years later, I still stayed in contact with her because she had taught these students and could give me the insight that I needed to connect with them.

After teaching for two years at the high school level, working on summer school projects, and sponsoring nearly every club activity available, I was asked by the principal of the school during the summer to consider becoming the Dean of Girls for the next year. That position required a master's degree which I was about to complete by commuting 125 miles one way, twice a week, after school was out in the afternoon. I accepted without asking too many questions. I found out that the job was really only classified as a half-time position. The other half of the day, I would teach. I was responsible for the discipline of the female students on a campus of 2,400 students. I was also assigned to ride various out-of-town school buses each week as the competitions occurred for our students. As with any half-time job put together with another half-time job, I really had two full jobs with very little support available. For this 7 a.m. to generally 10 p.m. job, I was paid a total of $300 more for the year than I would have made if I had been teaching full time. The experiences, however, were worth much more. I learned that not everyone taught with the commitment and energy with which I taught. Not everyone was concerned about the students' personal lives as I was. And, there were many who were. So, the bonding began with those who shared a common philosophy. We developed a system of peer coaching that very few people outside of our little group knew about because it was not the norm at that school. This was in the early 70s so all of the literature that labeled what we were doing had not yet hit our journals. But we know that we could be better teachers, and the only way we know to do it was to ask others to observe and give us feedback. The principals of the schools, at that time, did not do this anywhere in the district.

Since I had a master's degree by this time in English, I decided to apply for the position of Secondary English Supervisor when it became available. All of the supervisors' positions until that time had been held by men. I was the first woman to apply. When I got the job, the curriculum director told me that I had gotten the job because I was female, and they were afraid the Office of Civil Rights would become involved if they didn't have at least one woman among the five or six supervisors. I decided that I wouldn't become upset about that, because this would give me the chance to prove that I could do the job. Hopefully, it would prove to the administration at that time that women, in general, could do as well as, if not better than, men in this or similar jobs.

For nine years, I worked twice as hard, worked to implement twice as many innovations within the schools where I worked, and attended any training sessions I could to learn more and more about teaching and learning, and about curriculum, and how we can reconnect students who have become disillusioned with school. If a training session was offered, I was there. I did this job for nine years and learned a tremendous amount in the process.

I then had an opportunity to work with 41 school districts through a new job offered from our Regional Educational Service Center. The idea of working with that many school districts was exciting, so I accepted the job. I had an opportunity to work with some very bright people and to see the diversity among the school districts in our region. However, the thrill of seeing some project to completion was not there because all we did was to plant the ideas and water them. We were never able to enjoy the results. By this time, it was clear to me that I could not be very happy and fulfilled unless I was able to work with committed and dedicated people. I personally needed to know that others would "die on the Turkish wall" for certain educational purposes like I would. Therefore, I began to develop an informal list of characteristics that had to be present before I would invest my energy with a team.

I found such a team back with a district again and had the opportunity to become the Executive Director of Federal Programs and to help the newly hired assistant superintendent with staff development, which was my love. In that role I could make things happen for underprivileged children because of the federal monies. Also, the team that was created within the district was extraordinary. We were all mission-driven, committed to ALL children learning at an advanced level, and we all pushed ourselves to learn more about the teaching and learning process. It was the greatest professional time of my career. Many of the people who were part of that team and who have gone on to other jobs call back periodically and talk about how they have never found an environment like that since. We all miss that, because none of us have that at the moment to the extent that we had it then.

The superintendent was seeing the need for more and more staff development as the educational scene was changing so rapidly, so he asked me if I would be willing to start a new department within the district. It was another challenge, so I said yes and started the office of staff development within the district and began working with five different groups of personnel the first year and then ultimately 14 different groups, including everyone from custodial supervisors to the superintendent to design staff development programs that would equip them for the changing roles of schools. While I was in that job, that superintendent got an offer he couldn't refuse, and we got a new superintendent. The assistant superintendent left too, so I applied for the job. I got that job of assistant superintendent five years ago and am still holding that position.

Personal and Professional Landmarks

There have been two personal landmarks in my life: (1) the adoption of our son in 1980 and (2) the completion of my doctorate in 1990.

The first personal landmark, our son, has changed my whole outlook on life. He has been such a joy and had such a sense of humor that I know my life would not be nearly what it is today without him in it. The other landmark, the terminal degree, simply gave me the keener view that you can never know all there is to know in your field. I have continued to go to school after completing that degree so that I can continue to fill in the gaps in my own learning so that I can be a better problem solver as well as better innovator for the sake of our students. A day is lost only when we don't learn anything new. That is a tragedy.

The professional landmark that has made the biggest impact on me was the opportunity to work with the team that I described earlier. This team had total commitment. We had fun working together, we made the bad times for each other better, and we learned more about education and about people during that time than we had ever learned before or since.

Highest and Lowest Moments

The highest moments that I have had outside of working with the team that is described above have been when I have been conducting training sessions and I realize that I have every single person in the group (whether 20 or 200) with me

100 percent. When I can see the lights in their eyes and the smiles on their faces, I know that I have connected with them. That is very exciting.

My lowest moments have been connected with disappointments in other people when they put themselves first over the welfare of the organization or of other people. When I see committed, motivated people beat down by the politics of education or the myopia of others, I get very sad and very angry at the same time. I feel strongly that the innovators, the risk-takers are the people who will ultimately find the matches that make a difference for the most number of students. Sometimes these are the very people who are slapped in the face with barriers that should never be barriers. Those are my lowest and most frustrating moments.

Best and Worst Experiences

The very best experiences that I have had have been while learning new things with the team that was so special. When we worked long hours to learn about learning and then about leading others to that learning, it was the best of my experiences.

My worst experiences have tended to center around people or circumstances where I expected the people to do what was right. Instead, they decided to do what was the easiest or the most politically safe. That is when I see what could have gone down the drain. Those are my worst times.

Sources of Strength and Motivation

I find great strength and motivation in books. I read about people who have beat the odds to accomplish something special—usually for others. I read many leadership books about the skills and strategies and great leaders. I also read psychology books to learn how to better work with diverse populations. It is extremely motivating to read about how a leader helped an organization focus on continuous improvement, and how he used the ideas of everyone to improve the output and reputation of the company. When I use those same strategies with this organization, I see the results. This is motivating to me.

I also have a small group of people who share the same philosophy and general goals in life. They are tremendously strengthening to me. We get together periodically and share what we have learned and what we are reading. It's like a long distance study group.

Change of Women's Status

When I entered the profession, very few women were principals, and almost no women were superintendents. The tone at most schools was such that allowed the decisions to come from the top with no questions asked, and everyone just took care of their classrooms or offices. Little time for collaboration was needed because decisions were not collaborative in those days. The interesting thing is that most of us thought that was the way things were done best—because that's the only model that we had ever seen. For the most part, the hardball games were played by men because they knew the rules.

During the end of the 80s decade and during the 90s, things have changed. Many more women are in leadership roles, both as principals and as superintendents and assistant superintendents. The new school culture supports an environment that is collaborative. For the most part, that is the reason that I think that women's status has changed. Many women have the social expertise and the sensitivity to want to hear ideas from many sources. Most women are also not as ego-driven as some men are. These gender differences, I believe, have necessitated the change in women's status. Education has needed their skills and sensitivities in the 90s as education thought in the 60s and 70s that the strong upper hand was the better way.

In addition, the majority of the state's staff developers are women. The type of staff development that my district and other districts in the state have embraced is the type that teaches process through actual participation in the various processes. These staff developers are literally saving many people who started out in the strong upper hand times, and these administrators are extremely grateful for this new knowledge base. I know that I created my credibility with other district and state administrators, not because I had been an administrator for so many years, but because I taught others how to use group processes effectively. I am constantly called on to facilitate meetings, to resolve conflicts, to problem-solve with diverse groups. This knowledge base and the ability to listen well have changed the status of women in education.

Role Models, Mentors, and Sponsors

My first mentor was the librarian at the school where I did my student teaching. She must have seen something in me, because she quickly took an interest in me as a person and was instrumental in showing me the ropes that are generally not found by new teachers until much later. The next mentor I had was a classroom teacher in the same grade level where I was teaching. She helped me understand the adolescent and therefore enabled me to approach the student within, in order to teach him more effectively. She taught me lessons that I share with new teachers today, 24 years after I first learned them.

My first real educational role model came late in my career. A new superintendent and assistant superintendent came to the district. This pair shared my philosophy that all children can learn at advanced levels if we learn how to tap into them as whole people. I had never found administrators who believed that until 1986. Therefore, I really began to think that my philosophy was off track. It was like a new life when these two people asked me to join their team of central administrators because they were aware of my philosophy. We added two more people to the central team with a common philosophy and began involving staff and the community in the direction-setting for the district. We learned together. We debated hotly. We worked very long hours, but it paid off. We found many other staff within the district who shared our philosophy, but had learned how to keep it quiet like I had to survive. With the nucleus, we were able to change the culture of an organization and make the learning process for children much more positive and rewarding. When that superintendent left the district to take a job at a larger district, I actually experienced a period of mourning like I had not experienced in my life. The person that replaced him had none of the vision, few of the administrative skills, and was not courageous for the sake of the students. The couple of years that followed were the most frustrating of my entire career.

I have mentors today generally through a very dynamic support group of other men and women throughout the state who pride themselves on staying on the cutting edge of research and of practice. We meet in a retreat setting twice a year for a long weekend of study, reflection, and dialogue. We are a group of about 30 people, most of whom are assistant superintendents and staff developers. We are 95 percent female. When we return from these study groups, we all feel renewed and energized. We maintain fairly close contact during the periods between these retreats via telephone and fax. We also make it a point to let everyone know about unique training opportunities that are available throughout the state and try to get together during those occasions as well. Whether it is a group like this or a different kind of group or maybe even a single person, I feel strongly that everyone on the firing line must have a support system in order to maintain the perspective that we need to make the right decisions for the students within our schools.

Strategies to Improve
Communication Between the Genders

I am told that I am a good communicator and a good listener. I try to do those things well, which probably accounts for the perceptions. I think that the reason for the perception is my honesty and integrity. I have watched communication and trust spiral downward when people say one thing and do another. Communication that is honest and above board diminishes the gender gap. I also think it is important to ask for input and to respond to that input. When doors are left open and when egos don't create win-lose situations, genders have few, if any, problems with communication.

I also think that you must treat people with respect and honor their expertise. We really must nurture our people with the greatest talents, because it is through them that we may be able to save public education. When we treat people as people, and when we don't have different standards for men and women, communication has no problems. I believe that the other agendas that many of us bring with us [are] the culprit in the communication gap between the genders.

Specific Mentoring Strategies

I have used very specific mentoring strategies with several very talented people. Some of these people are female and some are male. Among these strategies that I'm aware of are the following:

1. Explaining how certain things work here
2. Actually teaching classes on various topics and processes that increase individuals' competencies
3. Sharing books and articles with them
4. Providing feedback after interviews or presentations to those who were interviewed or who presented certain strategies or processes. This is done only on request, of course.

The bottom line to mentoring, I think, is to care enough about the individual to share and to provide information to all those who could possibly need it. I find no good reason for withholding information from anyone just to increase the dependency of people on others. Information is power. Everyone ought to have it.

Advice to Women Aspiring to Educational Administration

My advice is clear: have a vision, construct a plan, take risks, and find a mentor. The vision and the plan will come only through interactions with others and reading and studying. Read, read, read. Always be a learner. I am convinced that all we need to know to make a difference for all children is available now. We just have to put the puzzle together in the right way. Therefore, we have to know more than we ever thought was possible to find the right match for children.

Don't be afraid to try something new. Say yes when you are not sure if you can, and celebrate when you accomplish the task. Always give credit to those who have helped you. Rarely is any task of quality accomplished by one person.

Find ways to learn or work with visionary people. If that is not possible, establish networks so that ideas can be shared and support can be provided. Be there to share and to support.

Establish priorities. Know when the focus is being lost because of activities that do not match the priorities or mission of the organization. Know when to ask questions to test whether or not some activity is diluting the focus of the organization.

Be positive, be reflective, and be kind. Education is a people business. Even if someone's contract has to be terminated, help them see that this is the best for them in the long run. Help them leave with dignity. These actions will establish you as a credible leader—one who talks the talk AND walks the walk.

Regrets

The only regret that I have ever had is that I was not more mobile. My husband's business is rooted in this location. I would have liked to have been able to search out superintendents like the one who was a role model for me. The greatest frustrations that I have experienced have come from the fact that I greatly miss the intellectual level, the activity level, the commitment level of that team that had only three years of work together. Once you've experienced that synergy, all other group dynamics pale by comparison.

Future Career Plans

I am considering taking a teaching position at the university in the city. They have contacted me several times to join their educational administration department so I could help mold the type of innovative, collaborative, and caring administrators that will be a necessity in the near future. Because they have begun to put together a team who are real practitioners, who go into schools and become a part of the school community, I might do that in a couple of years.

I have no aspirations to be a superintendent because of the politics associated with the position. I would not be able to make decisions just to keep my job when I know that the decision was not in the best interest of the students. I know how to avoid some frustrations, and this is one that I would avoid. I know that I can do more to affect the environment for students and staff in the position I'm in than in the superintendent's office.

8

Lesson 8: Lead by Example

Women can lead just as well as men, but they must work much harder to get to the same level.

I read many leadership books about the skills and strategies of great leaders.

The ability to facilitate meetings, to resolve conflicts, to problem-solve with diverse groups and to listen well have changed the status of women in education.

—*Elizabeth*

Power is part of the job, but it is not an end in itself.

—*Emily*

In the organization of tomorrow, claims Patterson in his work on leadership for today's schools, leading will become a process of influencing others to achieve mutually agreed-upon purposes for the organization (Patterson, 1993). Transformational leadership advocates participatory management that motivates others by transforming their self-interest into the goals of the organization. Transformational leaders are skilled in leadership patterns that inspire increased worker performance by encouraging all points of view (Langford, 1995). According to Loden, the leader effectively aids in facilitating agreement between opposing points of view to develop consensus problem-solving models (Langford, 1995). Rogers states that transformational leadership joins the "needs, values, and goals" of both leaders and followers (Langford, 1995). An issue integral to changing leadership perspectives is the restructuring efforts in schools (Beyer-Houda & Ruhl-Smith, 1995). Harrison, Killion, and Mitchell have defined one of the current restructuring efforts, site-based decision making, as a process that

> brings the responsibility for decisions as close as possible to the school . . . defining how school staffs can work collaboratively to make these decisions . . . creating ownership for those responsible for carrying out decisions by involving them directly in the decision-making process and by trusting their abilities and judgments. (Beyer-Houda & Ruhl-Smith, 1995, p. 43)

Another restructuring effort is referred to as systemic change. Unlike past reforms, which focused on changing components of the education system, systemic reform encompasses the impact of change on all aspects of the education system. Systemic reform therefore takes into consideration the interrelatedness of all the components that function together in the education system and realizes that as one component changes, so must the others to maintain the integrity, continuity, and consistency of the entire system (Slick & Gupton, 1993). Systemic reform is viewed as a shift from a more traditional educational system to one that emphasizes interconnectedness, active learning, shared decision making, and high levels of achievement for all students (Anderson, 1993). With the trends toward participatory style leadership and decentralization of power on the upswing, women's tendency toward a more integrative leadership style may actually be coming into vogue. Criswell and Betz (1995) further corroborate these changes as well as women's proclivity for participatory management:

> The trends toward site-based decision making and Total Quality Management in the nation's educational systems are signs that schools as a workplace are undergoing transformation. The new school environment calls for a new kind of administrator—"one who puts instructional issues in the forefront and one who solicits involvement of others in decision-making." Women's documented expertise in the areas of instructional leadership and empowerment should

serve as an asset to females who aspire to leadership positions in restructured educational environments. As a new
paradigm of leadership emerges, the unique strengths that
women administrators have displayed may give them an
advantage in the future. (p. 30)

Naisbitt and Aburdene (1990) predict that the 1990s will be the
breakthrough decade for women throughout corporate America. The
popular movement in the profession toward site-based/participa-
tory management at both the campus and central office levels has
given women hope that their more natural style of transformational
leadership might be appreciated and sought. Some authors suggest
that feminine leaders are well equipped to handle the emerging
problems of organizations because they possess the qualities of a
change agent with attributes of creativity, flexibility, and orientation
toward people rather than things (Langford, 1995; Shakeshaft, 1986b).
    Part of our research focused on finding out more about the
leadership characteristics of women leaders. There were 10 leadership
characteristics identified and used for study in our original questionnaire: aggression, competition, verbal orientation, spatial orientation, cooperation, motivated by power, concern about personal
relationships, career orientation, family orientation, and androgyny.
The purpose of this section was to determine the perceptions of
women in educational leadership positions regarding their own
leadership characteristics when compared with their male counterparts and when compared with other women in general. When comparing themselves with their male counterparts, the respondents
viewed themselves as more verbally oriented (50.7%), more concerned about personal relationships (62%), and more cooperative
(59.3%) than their male counterparts. They saw themselves as basically the same for the following characteristics: (a) aggressive (56%),
(b) competitive (51.3%), (c) spatially oriented (55.6%), (d) career oriented (50%), (e) family oriented (52%), and (f) androgynous (60.3%).
Note that 52% of the respondents felt that men in comparable positions were as family oriented as they were. This could be a reflection
of the more recent trend in this decade toward shared parenting in
the family unit typically brought on by both parents being employed
outside the home. The one characteristic that respondents indicated
they were less like men was "motivated by power" (64%). The three
characteristics that the women perceived themselves as possessing

more than men were characteristics of the transformational leadership style: more verbally oriented, more concerned about personal relationships, and more cooperative.

Terrence Deal contends that the movement toward participatory management involves transforming the basic character of schools (Lunenburg & Ornstein, 1991). He views schools as a culture and believes that the structures within the system or culture of public schools cannot be reformed—they must be transformed. This transformation would then, of necessity, change the basic character of the system being changed. Change is not easy under any circumstances, and public school systems are highly complex, surprisingly similar across the country, and very resistant to change (Holzman, 1993). Steven Berglas thinks the female style of leadership is better positioned for hard times: "In an era when the need to motivate is so important, women will do better because they are nurturers and value driven" (Billard, 1992, p. 70). Because educators are typically very skeptical of change, leaders in the profession will need to be highly skilled motivators to bring about the systemic changes needed. These leaders will also need to be people oriented and skillful at providing opportunities for the people they work with to participate in the decisions affecting their work lives, thereby giving them ownership in the change process.

In consideration of the systemic changes requiring a new vision of restructuring, leadership needs in public school education are evolving into more complex structures. Gardner is quoted in Langford (1995) as describing the talents of leaders with respect to six categories:

1. they think in the future;
2. they think global, rather than in analytical pieces and parts;
3. their influence is far reaching, even beyond the limits of their assigned followers;
4. they intuitively recognize the aura of leader and follower interaction;
5. they emphasize inspiration, motivation, and values; and
6. they strive to revitalize and change the current structure to deal with the demands of changing external or internal organization. (p. 100)

Many educational leaders believe that the type of leadership needed in public schools today is situational, and that neither transformational nor transactional leadership can be applied all of the time. This type of leadership is referred to as situational and is seen as more androgynous than either male oriented or female oriented in characteristics. The new vision of leadership is about a holistic, androgynous style (Langford, 1995). When the understanding of goals is clear and a consensus for expectations is present, sequential/rational methods, characteristic of the masculine, logical style, are easily used for charting the course of the organization; however, when administrators are looking for new ways to provide long-term education restructuring, the transformational, intuitive leadership styles, valued by females, become important (Norris, 1994). In our original survey, women respondents indicated that they were just as androgynous as their male counterparts. Various perspectives exist regarding the issue of androgyny and leadership. According to Friesen, androgyny stresses an inclusion of a broad repertoire and offers opportunities for men and women to engage in conflicts using those behaviors based on relevance (Tyree, 1995).

The women in our study reacted strongly to stereotypical statements regarding gender and leadership. When asked to respond to the following statements, our participants indicated as follows:

Women are perceived to be as powerful on the job as men—59% of the women either disagreed or strongly disagreed with this statement.

Women are more sensitive to people matters than men—80% of the women indicated they agreed or strongly agreed.

Women are not as effective in their decision-making as men—98% of the women either disagreed or strongly disagreed with this statement.

Women are incapable of financial finesse—95% of the women responding either disagreed or strongly disagreed.

Women lack delegation skills—94% of the respondents disagreed or strongly disagreed.

Women are frequently perceived in stereotyped roles—86% of the respondents either agreed or strongly agreed with the statement.

Women lack political savvy—85% of the respondents disagreed or strongly disagreed.

Women in administration are more people-oriented than men in admin-istration—68% indicated that they agreed or strongly agreed with the statement.

Women are not good mediators—92% of the women disagreed or strongly disagreed with this statement.

It is obvious that these women administrators do not see them-selves as the typical stereotyped female, nor do they like to be perceived that way. On the other hand, they are not completely adopting male leadership characteristics in order to be successful leaders. Perhaps this is further evidence that the leadership for tomorrow's schools will be more situational and androgynous in nature. One female administrator in another study commented:

You have to establish your own identity, show your own values and must not be confrontive or abrasive to prove yourself. I do not try to be the manly, tough person. Some men resent it when women try to be more "male." I am who I am! Genuineness and credibility cannot be an act. (Funk, 1995, p. 68)

Transformational leadership is viewed as fusing the integration of culturally accepted masculine and feminine roles. Although the fa-cilitating skills inherent in transformational leadership may come more naturally to females because of early socialization patterns, males as well as females use transformational styles successfully (Langford, 1995).

In the final part of the original survey, which dealt with leader-ship characteristics, respondents were asked to "comment briefly on whether you believe women have as much leadership potential as men." The following are a few of the comments made in response to this statement by our top-level female administrators:

We have the same potential. The leadership I exert now is more that of cooperation—encouraging people to participate in decision making. (Superintendent)

I believe women have as much leadership potential as men. However, I do believe women often approach leadership differently. (Different is different, not better or worse.) Some leadership styles are more effective in specific situations— I'm not certain that it is gender related. (Superintendent)

Women definitely have as much if not more leadership potential in most if not all areas. Women tend to be more nurturing, caring, and understanding. They tend to listen more and encourage more participation than men. . . . They are more democratic. (Principal)

Definitely as much as men—more action oriented as a rule; more organized, more caring. (Superintendent)

Women have the same abilities to become powerful leaders. They can work well with teams of people. They are not so concerned with the power relationships as men are. They are also hard workers and can accomplish tasks more efficiently. (Assistant superintendent)

These comments reflect the characteristics of transformational leadership. They also touch on the prospect that good leadership is not gender specific. Knowing and believing this from the female perspective, however, does not make the road to the top any easier; for as we know, there are still many who advocate the transactional, male-dominated style of leadership as the only "right way" to provide leadership. Be aware that there are many women as well as men who still cater to this type of leadership.

Leadership characteristics and styles of leadership are frequently addressed in the stories of the 15 women in this book. Emily commented on the above-mentioned statement, "You believe women have as much leadership potential as men":

Sure! Women are able to lead. Men too are able to lead. Style is the key here. The traditional leadership role came from power and bluster. Good leaders don't need the swaggering power. The best leadership doesn't come from those who lust after power.

Through the stories told by the 15 female administrators in our study, there are commonly perceived characteristics of leadership and expertise that emerge. Consensus builder, collaborator, team builder, shared decision-making, valuing of individual participation, role modeling, goal setting, good communicator, hard worker, fair, consistent, maintains integrity, believes in self and others, works toward providing the best possible education for children, and positive outlook and enthusiastic motivator are but a few mentioned. Marie, a superintendent in the Northwest, represents the others well when she says:

> I am not a charismatic leader, or a leader of any personal power. I am not an articulate speaker, but I am a risk taker who will attempt difficult tasks to advance toward a worthwhile goal. I am persistent in the district's mission; I have a strong value system and a rich variety of experience. I have learned much about building consensus from my experiences, and I am comfortable sharing leadership with staff members, the school board, and patrons. I credit my knowledge of consensus building to my association with other women in leadership positions.

Although there is humility expressed in what she relates, one still has the feeling that the humility arises not so much from any lack of professional expertise as from her valuing of others' opinions and abilities to contribute to the grander scheme of what is best for the children of the school district. She states further that

> our society teaches behaviors or skills to women that enable them to be different leaders from the traditional male figurehead. Women have always been able to use these skills to get things done. Now, America is learning that a leader does not have to be dominant, authoritative, or male.

Frequently, these women administrators referred to difficult times during their respective tenures in their school districts. More often than not, these conflicts were brought on by political battles that somehow seemed to forget the major charge of all persons involved—to provide the best possible education and guidance for students in the district. Freda (interim superintendent in the Northeast) speaks of the damage that can be wrought in the political arena that affects public schools:

I am well aware that my political naïveté created problems for me, and that I clearly did not have the backing I needed of some key players. For this, I must look at how I did not meet up to the political challenge. The shame, however, is that I truly was working wonderfully well with the teachers, parents and administrators, and wonderful things were happening for kids in the district as a result.

Brenda (superintendent in the Northeast) corroborates Freda's experience in her story:

The old adage that it is very hard to see the forest for the trees is applicable. I never wanted to believe I had less opportunity than the men. I never wanted to believe the cards were stacked against me. I never wanted to believe that when push comes to shove people can be mean, base and self-serving. I never wanted to believe people would almost kill to maintain power and control independent of right or wrong. But those were childish and unrealistic principles. At mid-life, in my case, I learned about the realities of life.

Brenda was an accomplished leader. She relates:

I was successful as a superintendent because I grew and learned at a very rapid pace during my three years in the position. The job involved skills of leadership which included independence, creativity, political savvy, interdependence, decision-making, breadth of knowledge, risk-taking, confidence and competence. . . . Leadership and modeling are about being a learner.

Of all the stories shared by the women administrators, Emily's (assistant superintendent in the West) seemed to encompass best the many issues facing these women as leaders in the profession. Whether or not they realize it, their experiences within their own districts and through this book are providing aspiring female administrators examples of what to expect, what to do, and what not to do to reach the top. Emily's story describes beautifully her journey to the top with some ups and downs. Throughout, she is wonderfully reflective, and we are able to see the development of an outstanding professional administrator. As is true with all of our women, she remains true to her convictions, believing that she can make a difference for children. She is an obvious people person who struggles to understand others who do not seem to value the importance of the profession as much as she does. She experiences some very rewarding relationships with a mentor and some coworkers that are heartening and speak to all of us for the need for advocates in our lives.

Emily's Story

Reflecting on Now

Time softens many of the hard edges. I am fifty-one. I became an administrator in public schools in 1974. My current position is as assistant superintendent in a K-12 district. I believe it is the "perfect job"—or at least nearly perfect.

Joe, my superintendent, and I work as a team. Few superintendents will allow the type of relationship we have to emerge. In another time, in another district, I worked with a superintendent who would not allow anyone else power, or even significant access to the decision-making process. Joe is different.

Joe has spent his entire career in this district. He became superintendent about eight months before I was hired. Joe presented two or three final candidates to the governing board and I was their selection. This is his way of doing things. I believe from the first interview, he thought we could work well together, and the board selected me. (He even saved the tape of my interview and gave it to me.)

Joe is a nice looking man with the build of the distance runner that he was in college. I am taller than he is. Sometimes being a tall woman is a disadvantage, particularly with a shorter boss. Not with Joe.

After the hell of working with insecure men, Joe is a great blessing. He delights in the positive accomplishments of staff members. He encouraged me to get back with my dissertation, despite the fact that he does not have a Ph.D. A good match is critical in a close working relationship.

One morning, Joe and I were discussing how a principal (male) and an assistant (female) were locked in a disintegrating relationship. He asked, "What do you do that makes our relationship work?" It is what both of us do. We communicate about professional and personal things. We respect each other's opinions and professional knowledge and experience. Joe and I are a team, yet I respect when he leads. He is the superintendent. He takes the major heat. As he asked another time, teasingly, "Why is it that I do the miserable stuff and you have the fun?"

Path

I wanted to be a foreign service officer. My undergraduate training and initial graduate work was directed toward that goal. I had a mentor who encouraged me. He believed I could do anything I wanted to do. Much like my dad and mom, Leon also was a retired career diplomat.

As I began work on a Ph.D. in history, I met James. I weighed marriage and a career selection that, at the time, negated marriage with children. We married. He was still in school. I started substituting. I had taught college history as a TA, so I substituted in secondary. After a few days of successful substituting in a lower socioeconomic area, I was offered a regular job. I would teach English, although my major was social science. The latter field was reserved for men!

Teaching high school was great. I loved it and the kids were the prize. Eventually, I even was allowed to teach a social science course. I developed one of the first minorities courses in our state. It was terrific. The multiracial group of students I taught were challenging. They taught me to be a teacher—and a diplomat!

Recruited to return to graduate school and work with teacher interns, I had new challenges. I wanted to know why some things worked and others did not. Professional literature, current practice, and more became my passion. Along the way, my university advisor said, "Emily, where your career is going, you need an elementary credential." I wondered where he thought I was going, but I must not have expressed that too loudly. He continued, "I have arranged for you to student teach kindergarten in the mornings at the lab school. Mary (my daughter) will have a tuition waiver there."

Great! My career was going somewhere and I was expected to teach little kids. I could be a curriculum person without actually working with those gooey-handed kids, couldn't I? Wrong—at least in my advisor's mind. It was fun, and I started seeing connections between the older kids' needs and the needs of the younger ones. He was right. A curriculum person needs to be more global. A secondary curriculum specialization, I discovered, is an anachronism.

While in graduate school, I was able to design components for teacher education programs. I administered the summer session and did other administrative tasks. When I left graduate school, I had full teaching credentials for elementary and secondary, plus an unrestricted administrative credential. I accepted a job creating and running a hospital school for troubled youths (ages 10 through 21).

Two years of learning about special education and designing programs was further preparation for wherever my career was going. Now with two children and still a graduate scholar husband, I sought a post as an administrator in public school. We moved to a beach city in our state, where I was assistant principal.

My first principal was asked to leave at the end of the year. It was another learning experience. The second principal was wonderful. He was a mentor. When cutbacks were announced, he encouraged me to move on. "Two years as an AP are enough. Apply for secondary principalships." I did.

The position I accepted was in a beautiful small mountain community in the northern part of our state. While many people believed that the intent of my hiring was to get the Office of Civil Rights out of the district's business, I did not believe that. I was in the largest school in the district. It also was the most visible, and the district office was in the same town. Every day, the superintendent, at about 4 p.m., would come to the school and run on our track. It was exciting and difficult for a young woman principal. The faculty was mostly male. The logging town itself was not well prepared for a woman high school principal, particularly one who was married and with young children.

The high school had a few women on the faculty—a home ec. teacher, a p.e. teacher, a librarian, and three English teachers—fewer than 17 percent. We hired a woman counselor shortly after my arrival. The faculty culture was male. They even had a traditional "retreat" that was a rite of the late summer, with lots of beer and comradeship. Spouses were not welcome. I did not attend. Occasionally, one or two of the women would, but it basically was a male party.

Naive as I was, I expected to make connections with others and establish a good working relationship. I had been respected at my previous schools and felt I could do the job well. Never had I been accused of not being a people person. The staff at HS was different, however. The culture was set. Teachers were accustomed to doing their own thing. For several years, they had been in transition. Many assumed I would be there for one year and move—or be moved—on.

I expected some of the faculty women to like me, and maybe even enjoy having a woman in leadership. (Remember, this was in the mid-'70s.) What a shock it was to find no loyalty and little support. The counselors and the assistant principal were terrific, but many of the teachers were, it seemed, not inclined to accept leadership from a woman. And the women teachers were even less inclined! I grew up thinking that if I just worked a little harder, things would work out fine. So I worked harder—and harder.

My schedule was to report to my office at 5:30 a.m. I seldom left campus during the extended school day, except to take a student home or to run something to the District Office. Janice, the cafeteria manager, often sent up a lunch for me just before she left for the day at about 2 p.m. If she had not seen me by then, she knew I had not eaten.

I moved about the campus through the day. One teacher, complaining or complimenting, noted, "She doesn't slow down." If no event was scheduled for the evening, I would leave by 5:30 p.m. More frequently, I would go to the gym and watch a volleyball game or basketball scrimmage. I went to over 90 percent of the events, whether cultural or athletic.

I saw every play and every concert. I learned to enjoy all the sporting events. Often, my husband and children would join me. All too frequently, dinner would be food from the snack bar grill. Twice monthly, I was at governing board meetings. A typical week was at least 60 hours, and usually, due to sports, more like 70. The weeks were long and required me to be moving, moving, moving. Occasionally, I was invited to staff get-togethers, but not to the local club or other meet-at-the-watering-hole gatherings.

Several times, cartoons with biting labels about women in leadership, or those attacking my religion were found on the teacher bulletin board. Sometimes, I saw them. Other times, they were taken down by someone else. I had several people who admired my work ethic and who tried to support and help me.

Like any new administrator, I had successes and failures. I worked those long hours and went to hundreds of school events seeking to become a real leader in the school. After my first year, although I did not know it yet, the move to have me out of the school was well underway. Years later, several people told me the superintendent had said I would only be there a year to solve the Office of Civil Rights problem. My reports were returned with commas and other superficial grammatical corrections, even though the "corrections" were style comments and not errors. Other, less literate principals were not given this special attention. Even when no other principal had a particular project completed, I was still singled out for not getting it in yet. I was called upon to trade a strong teacher for a weak one when another principal was in trouble, yet I was considered less than adequate by the superintendent when I could not get a high level of performance out of a veteran teacher who was perennially poor. I was asked to evaluate out people who had been called superior in formal evaluations by the prior administrator, yet considered mediocre or worse by that individual and the superintendent. I fired two teachers who needed to be taken out, but was called weak by the superintendent.

A fine teacher, who was a veteran of over 24 years and had been the informal leader of the faculty, commended me for my courage and honesty in those firings. The superintendent, too, said he was impressed with my ability to evaluate and remove the teachers. To me, he questioned whether anyone else could have done this, yet he did not include such positive statements in my evaluations.

The superintendent even suggested that I should evaluate out my wonderful colleague and friend, assistant principal John. That suggestion was accompanied by the off-hand comment that he could be replaced by a particular individual, a teacher who was a favorite of the superintendent. John was a great assistant principal. He was even responsible for helping the superintendent get his first position in our district. The super was not known for his loyalty.

Different standards of performance were expected of me than of my male colleagues, and different perks were given. Wives of administrators were hired by the district if they held teaching credentials. My husband applied and was not hired. The rumor was that we did not need the second income. Another rumor was that it just was not right to have a woman making more than her husband in the district. It seemed strange. The district encompassed most of the county, so James was not able to teach and live in our area. He had to find other work. Vacations were interesting too. I was told that my assistant principal or I must be in town or nearby at all times, even during the summer or on weekends. I was not to leave without having the plant "covered," just in case. Other principals left for periods of time without the same proviso.

An error in the eyes of some was that I did have two children while being principal. I did not miss even a day of work through the pregnancies and even the deliveries. In fact, I did not slow my 10 to 12 hour everyday pace. The boys both were born in the summer at a local hospital. (Gee, I didn't even leave town!) After the birth of one, I had to hurry and prepare for a major board presentation at a governing board meeting that was held in another city within the district. The presentation could have been done at any time, but the superintendent scheduled it then. His secretary tried to get it changed. He said he realized it could be done at another time, but he wanted it to be presented on that date and in that place. I did a razzle-dazzle presentation while the baby was in the car with his dad, waiting for the meeting to conclude.

One day, while pregnant, I climbed into our four-wheel-drive truck. My superintendent commented, "I'll bet the others could not do what you are doing." The truck was high. Some of the other principals were short. I just smiled and waved. What did he mean? I was naive. He had a plan to get me out, but I did not realize his cunning.

I was told by several people that the exit plan was devised over a long period. My knowledge that things were really bad came with an evaluation, then a meeting. Willy came into my office. "I understand Ellen (my secretary) is not working full days since her operation."

"She is working seven and a half hours as required." Ellen usually worked 10 or so hours without any overtime slips. Her husband had an in-town job and they rode together. She worked to keep herself occupied until he came to get her.

"Ellen is not working a normal shift and you are covering for her."

"She is working a split shift. Her doctor said she needed to get back to work immediately. He said if she did not, she might lose the will to live. He said cancer is like that. Working is good therapy."

"But she is not working a normal day."

"True. She has some therapy mid-morning, then returns."

"Put her on disability."

"But she doesn't want it and neither does her doctor."

"Then evaluate her out."

"What?"

"Get her out of here."

The conversation went on. I refused to comply with his request. It was morally wrong. Willy left angry with me. It was not the first time he had asked me to do something morally, ethically, or legally wrong. But is was the most difficult. I clearly told him I would not comply, despite his finger waving in my face.

An undercurrent developed. There were people suspicious of me. Fire two teachers, even if they deserve it, and you get a backlash. The rivulet became a river, then a torrent. The superintendent, according to several sources, unleashed the dam by promising one individual—the person he suggested as assistant if I would only get John out of the way—an administrative post if he would rally the forces against me. The ground upon which I stood was soon sodden and unstable.

"If you were not a woman and a Mormon, this would not be happening to you." The superintendent actually said that to me! He also told me I was an excellent administrator but he did not have confidence in my ability to be firm and to lead in that school. He said he did not need to have any reason other than that to replace me.

At about the same time, the assistant superintendent said I was the best administrator in the district. I believe he heard the gender and religious remark and I said, "So what does that get me?" He just smiled.

Several good teachers, and some who were not the best, supported me. They went to the superintendent and were greeted with disinterest. A small group tried to meet with the governing board. They were granted a short meeting, but it was to no avail. The board members generally were "in the pocket" of the superintendent.

When the board meeting came, my strong supporter was not present. He was "ill" according to the roll call statement. I was reassigned to an undesignated spot. One option, designed to maintain the Office of Civil Rights at bay, was in a district office assignment using my special education background.

The choice of the superintendent was to send me to a 5th grade class. It was a specially selected class of over 30 students, including behavior problem children and some with serious learning difficulties. My neighbor had 24 students. Interesting.

I had a great year with these children. It was a healing time and a fun time. They grew and so did I. The district continued to give me negatives. Eventually, the assignment game became too much for me. I quit. I pulled out my retirement, since my husband's business venture was not doing well. I wanted out of public education.

I wrote, messed with my dissertation, and did some radio news. I cared for our children. Finally, it was obvious that I needed to work again. Applying for jobs from having no job is tough. My approach sparked a fair amount of interest. Eventually, I was interviewed for an ideal curriculum position. The superintendent and interview panel liked me. Then I met with the board. It was a match.

Where Did All My Colleagues Go?

A hurtful thing was when my colleagues deserted me. I had been the organizer, the doer, and the good friend. Yet when I was tainted, they were gone. I was the only woman administrator in the district. I was the first woman high school administrator. When named, I was 31 and there were only a handful of women heading comprehensive high schools in the entire state. But I was a team player. I helped my colleagues. I did my part and more, without taking credit. The men, with the exception of Dan—my assistant principal—deserted me. There was no support or even expression of concern.

A digression:

Dan applied for the principalship when I did. He was a W.W.II veteran, a long time teacher, coach, and v.p., as well as a fixture in the community. John did not get the position and I was concerned. I went to his office shortly after arriving and said, "We need to talk."

John smiled, got up, closed the door, and quietly said, "The super and the board wanted you. They did not want me. It is okay."

I started to speak, but he shook his head.

"Look, Emily, their decision has nothing to do with our relationship. If you will give me one or two things, I will be the best vice-principal you could have."

Startled, I asked, "What?"

"First, let me give you my opinions and ideas before you make a decision and when that is possible. Second, let's talk behind closed doors, so that when a decision is made, we are united." I just nodded. He continued, "If you can listen to me and value my thoughts, I can be completely loyal. If I don't believe something is right, I'll tell you—behind closed doors."

I watched this man and gauged his age. He was old enough to be my father. He watched me, too. "John, what you ask is fair. It's the right thing to do. I'm sort of amazed that the board . . ."

John cut me off. "We can't speculate about the board, Emily. You are the principal. I think my job is to help us be a great team."

The beginnings of a relationship were laid. John was true to his word. He was and is a great person. He taught me, cajoled me, and followed me. He never challenged my leadership and he sought to make me into the best principal I could be. I owe a great deal to Dan.

A few months ago, I visited with John and told him how important his tutoring was to my personal and professional growth. I told him that I love and respect him. We both became teary.

Regrets, Suggestions

Saying thanks:

I regret that I did not say thanks to some of the people who helped me early on. I suppose I always anticipated he or she would be there next week, next month, next year. As I press on in my career, I try to thank those who are kind or who go the second mile. Specific, timely appreciation works for kids, and it also is great for adults.

Being right is often being wrong:

Being right often is unimportant. As a new curriculum administrator, I was engaged in a "war" to get a new K-8 text series into our schools. It was math adoption year. The best text was manipulatively based. The teachers had narrowed the selection to two. One was good. The other was awful, but more like what we had done for years. Nine people were on the committee, including me. The positions had been taken—four to four. I was the only administrator. I could cast the tie-breaking vote. Wisdom prevailed. "I will not be using this series in the classroom. This must be decided by you. I will be in my office working on the paper mountain. Please let me know when you are ready with a decision."

I walked out. Over an hour later, the decision had been made. It was not—in my view—the right one, but it was done. (I avoided being the bitch/witch, too.) A little ray of hope was the suggestion that a dual adoption at K-2 be done, to allow teachers who wanted another manipulatively based option that opportunity. Okay, I gave the freedom to choose. They selected the old approach. I had lost the battle, but with some grace.

Later, teachers began asking for additional inservice in the manipulative approaches. The requests for workshops were increasing. Teachers were paying for one-week sessions themselves. Materials requests were choking the system. It took seven years, but the teachers were changed. Drill and kill is rare. Pattern blocks, attribute blocks, base ten sets, tiles, cubes, etc. are all in neat bins or piled on the tables with active children solving problems.

I did not win the war—we all did. Children are becoming mathematically powerful, due to the greater understanding they and their teachers have acquired through teaching and learning with manipulatives. Had I forced the adoption of a series many teachers feared, this would not have occurred. Math phobias and the DDO (Damn District Office) Syndrome would have combined forces. Oh yes, I do praise those pioneers with manipulatives and the courageous ones who stepped out and took the workshops. They get the credit and I learned a great lesson.

Interestingly, several strong teachers were watching to see how I handled this issue. They had not supported me or my position. They did not trust me, but were willing to give them a bit more room now. I was not going to throw around my power. Women must be particularly careful in wielding power—more careful than the men. Gentle, patient approaches combined with an ability to stand up on important issues will win.

Mentoring women and others:

"Emily, you seem to favor women in your mentoring," said my superintendent one afternoon. It was true. I started to protest the statement, but could not.

"Let me think about that and respond later," I requested. As I thought about the charge, I wondered why. The more I reflected, the more I understood. Men in our district talk on the golf course or while drinking a beer. They share little about feelings and deep concerns. I suspect, having read some of the material about the ways men and women approach feelings, this is common.

Early in my career when I had a male mentor, he told me things and asked me to think about things. Seldom did he ask me what I thought and felt. Frequently, he shared his knowledge and understandings about situations. He was and is a wonderful human being, but it always remained difficult to open up to him and express any inadequate feelings. He did not know how to deal with those concerns. It was almost as if he wanted to say, "Come on, be a mensch."

When I compliment a male principal and seek to open communication, often he will seem worried about what is coming next. He may deflect the compliment with humor, or even an aggrandizing statement. A woman principal might smile and say, "I tried to make that work. What else did you notice?"

Routinely, I receive more advice and counsel calls from the women principals. The men may need the same advice and counsel, but usually do not ask.

Joe and I discussed my thoughts later. We made some strategy plans based on what both of us perceived. He values my observations; I value his. Joe is a mentor to me. He encourages my mentoring others, regardless of gender. I still am learning.

I believe I have a special obligation to support and encourage women and other under-represented groups in

becoming administrators. (My definition of under-represented includes people who are willing to sacrifice in behalf
of kids, so that definition includes good people regardless of
gender, race, or ethnicity.) This obligation goes beyond the
boundaries of my district or my county.

A mentoring relationship which I have had for several
years is with a younger male administrator who has had two
negative situations as an assistant principal to a woman
principal. He has fine qualities and is avoiding making the
lack of success in those two circumstances a gender issue. I
remain as near as the phone for him when he has questions
or just wants to share. Part of mentoring is listening to the
good things and giving the "atta-boy" or "atta-girl" support.
We get too little of that. Since we get too little, maybe it means
we need to give it out more. (Could this be the mentoring
version of casting bread upon waters?)

And what about me?

When I need some of this support, I have one or two people
I can call. I have learned to ask. "Lisa, this is one of those
days. Will you have some time later?" She makes the time.
The calls go both ways. We both have learned that sharing
burdens lightens them. There are days I must lighten the load
before I can go home, even if that means going home an hour
later. I still have young children there and they need a mom
who is together.

Ride a bike with your kids. Hike. Do yard sales. Cruise
museums. Canoe. Take time for yourself and your family.
The job is not worth being a second rate person, mother and
wife.

Additionally, I take time to be quiet. I must nurture my
spirit. I must feed it and cultivate it.

Gonna climb that mountain:

Choose the mountain upon which you will die. Be prepared
to move to another district or another state even. You must
realize that you serve on a year-to-year basis. A board
changes, the superintendent changes, or the political climate

changes and administrators are dumped. I have a list of personal goals and personal objectives. These relate to me and who and what I am. Politics or my job will not cause me to change those goals.

Personal integrity is paramount. I stood in a packed auditorium presenting an unpopular plan to parents. In the front row was a teacher, a very good teacher. She did not like the message. She was expressing her dismay and citing information that was not true. The hall was primarily parents. Many knew this teacher. As a lull in my presentation came and another was talking, I leaned over and said, "The information you are presenting is not correct. I don't want to make you appear unknowledgeable, or to make myself look foolish." She protested for a second. "Have I ever lied to you?" She noted I had not. "I am not now. Let's get together tomorrow and I'll show you the data." She became quiet. She let me finish my presentation. She asked later for the further information. She cut me quarter then, but I had better never have an integrity lapse, or she never will again. The contemporary Russian poet Yevgeny Yevtushenko said during the Soviet era:

How sharply our children will be ashamed
taking at last their vengeance for these horrors
remembering how in so strange a time
common integrity could look like courage.

I have had to reach down into my deepest resources several times in my career and demonstrate the sort of courage that could have been a front-page newspaper story (but never was). Daily, I must show integrity.

I promised myself decades ago that no job would cause me to violate my personal ethics. I will die upon that mountain—or I will bring others to my mountaintop.

High on a mountaintop:

Sometimes bringing others to your mountaintop will require patience and endurance beyond what you believe you have. Impatience is part of each of my personal failures. Patience is part of each of my personal successes. Wisdom is knowing when to exercise extraordinary patience and endurance. If I had my experience in that small mountain community to live over again, I would exercise greater patience and endurance.

My superintendent notes that one of my strengths is waiting. He claims that I get almost anything I want, because I am willing to wait. While that is not completely true, there is a lot to being willing to wait. Impatience in a woman is not accepted as a positive quality.

Speaking of qualities:

A man who presses to get things done is called a strong leader. A woman who demonstrates the same aggressiveness is called a bitch or a pushy broad. I still see the hesitation to accept in women "go-getter" qualities.

Lusting after power:

Some things I have noticed about many people, especially men in administration, is the concern for gaining power. As I have matured, I have found several things. One is that the trend toward participatory management often gives messages of weakness. Women imbued with this concept in graduate training usually come off as weak. A woman asking everyone what they think is frustrating and vexing for many. A man may be seen in a different way. Finding the middle ground is a key to success for most women. She must chart a middle course between being a bitch and clueless.

I like to make decisions quietly, asking for advice long before it is needed. People like to sense their opinions are of value, yet most teachers want knowledgeable leadership. In my district, that middle ground is comfortable for me.

We have a wonderful program in our first grade at a chapter 1 school. I listened to our three good first grade teachers over the years. They wanted to spend more time encouraging children to write and publish their books, yet class size and time would not allow this activity. Gathering their wants and combining them with multimedia computers, I started generating an idea for a program using well-prepared instructional specialists under the direction of the teachers. Asking the counsel of those teachers occasionally ensured that they viewed the programs as theirs. They own it now that it is a reality. The success belongs to them, the instructional specialists, and the children. My job was to make things happen, enabling these teachers to do the extra things they wanted to and more, without burdening them.

Power itself is not a motivator for me. I want to accomplish things for the good of children. Seldom is my motivation brought into question, since I do not get into the power game. Actually, my power base is stronger because I can accept advice, make decisions—and change when needed—and because I listen.

Joe, my superintendent, is a good model, too. The board thanked him for something well done. He smiled and said, with some pride, "Charles (maintenance supervisor) and Emily did that. I will convey your appreciation." They who lust after power seldom do this, yet it is a very powerful act. Others are given credit; Joe looks good, too. Used sincerely, this gives power to good leadership.

I believe our motivations follow us. Watching colleagues is illustrative. A teacher leader noted, "He (a principal) is concerned about his power; she (another principal) is concerned about doing a good job for the kids."

"So who has the most power?" I asked.

"In the long run, she does."

Occasionally, I must directly exercise power. I fired two teachers when I was a principal. I have written people up when needed. I have called others on the carpet. I removed a long-term classified employee. I have said no and stuck to it. As I have matured in my profession, I have learned how to handle this wielding of power without getting caught up in my righteousness. Power is part of the job, but it is not an end in itself.

Emily's experiences as related in her story clearly illustrate the many obstacles and triumphs that women face in the profession as they climb the ladder toward leadership positions. She reaches out to assist others, only to lose their support at a later time. Whether this is an example of human frailty or an intentional lack of support under fire will probably never be known. It is a very real situation, and it definitely had an impact on her professional career. One has to wonder, though, if those persons who were not supportive of her when the "chips were down" would have reacted the same way had she been a male high school principal.

The education profession desperately needs to tap the leadership potential among the qualified and credentialed women available to the profession. Over the past decade, the literature and research regarding women in educational administration has focused increasingly on what needs to happen to improve the quality of leadership in education for everyone irrespective of gender. Now, at the onset of systemic reform, the education profession can no longer set aside or discourage professional women who are invaluable resources and available to assist with and lead the type of change processes needed for successful systemic change. As the total system changes, so must its attitude about women in leadership positions in the profession. The socialization barriers of the past that locked women out of administrative positions because they were viewed as being too sensitive, indecisive, conforming, dependent, and nonassertive must be put aside. First of all, the women responding to both phases of the research upon which this book is based often do not reflect stereotypical characteristics of women in general. But more importantly, the very leadership characteristics that women typically possess are those that are so often needed by the profession to bring about desirable changes. Research shows that logical and intuitive decision-making styles are not specific to gender but may be specific to situations, work environment, or the leader's organizational position (Langford, 1985; Shakeshaft, 1986a). Truly, school administration is a holistic process that requires both logical and intuitive styles of leadership. Transformational leadership embodies those needed characteristics and is the type of leadership typical of most women. The transformational model is woven from balanced thought patterns of knowledge, inspiration, and feeling (Langford, 1995). By combining rationality or knowledge by experiences with individual consideration of others, transformational leaders use both masculine and feminine styles to lead others (Langford, 1995). Both men and women are frequently comfortable with the transformational leadership style. Therefore, it is important that a variety of human potentials be given equal access to and even sought for filling today's tough leadership positions. The women and men exploring and defining transformational leadership are offering a vital and increasingly successful option for change (Billard, 1992). As transformational leadership settles into our schools, the results should be a more productive and humane workplace for everyone concerned. The profession should no longer be concerned about the gender of the person in the leadership position but should be focused on a leadership relationship that brings about the best possible educational experiences for the students. There should exist within each school environment an appreciation and respect for the qualities, skills, and expertise that the *individual* male or female administrator brings. Masculine characteristics, feminine characteristics, and some neutral characteristics with effective leadership interaction give a new perspective, one of *androgyny*, where performance is judged according to its "rightness" for a particular situation rather than by gender identity (Tyree, 1995). We need the best of the best in our profession to take us forward and to meet the challenges of educating young people in the future. A key to this future success in the profession is effective communication among all involved. Elizabeth (assistant superintendent in the Southwest) astutely shares the significance of communication upon the future of the success of transformational leadership.

> Communication that is honest and above board diminishes the gender gap. I also think it is important to ask for input and to respond to that input. When doors are left open and egos don't create win-lose situations, genders have few, if any problems with communication and working together.
>
> I also think that you must treat people with respect and honor their expertise. We really must nurture our people with the greatest talents (male or female), because it is through them that we may be able to save public education. When we treat people as people, and when we don't have different standards for men and women, communication has no problems. I believe that the other agendas that many of us bring with us are the culprits in the communication gap between the genders.

Nell (assistant superintendent from the Southeast) sums up the situation nicely. She states, "I truly believe that in this business, one works with people, not for them, no one person owns a district. We all, male and female, are in this business together and our product is the student."

9

The Evolution of Issues Related to Leadership and Gender

Even though the numbers of female administrators in education are greater than they have ever been, they remain significantly underrepresented as a gender—especially when you consider that they make up more than 70% of the whole profession. Also, a closer analysis of where today's women administrators are geographically located and of their salaries reveals a pattern of smaller districts and comparatively less pay than male administrators (Gupton & Slick, 1994). Historically, explanations offered for the underrepresentation of women in educational administration include women's lack of aspiration for administrative positions and the inadequate preparation and qualification of many women for administration coupled with their lack as a gender of natural leadership ability. Over time, many of the circumstances that supported these explanations for women's lack of equitable representation in educational administration have changed significantly and have resulted in several major shifts in the explanations for women's continued underrepresentation in the field. These shifts must be more widely acknowledged in order to provide women with the kinds of support and help they need to continue to improve their status in the workplace.

Important, too, is the need to expand the focus given to entry-level concerns to include on-the-job performance and retention issues regarding women administrators in the profession. Although entry-level concerns are still warranted, the increasing numbers of women gaining administrative positions have created a need to look at how they are faring in these leadership positions. The women in our survey revealed a host of complex problems related to women in top-level positions. Some of these issues include the importance of

looking at *where* these positions are located, how much power
these titles and positions actually reflect, and how today's women
administrators' salaries compare with the salaries of their male counterparts. The evolution of the issues surrounding educational leadership and gender merit candid acknowledgment and greater explo-
ration than are offered in the literature or in most discussions on
gender equity. These shifts—as we interpreted them and as exempli-
fied throughout the book—are summarized into the following
themes in this chapter in an effort to reinforce critical information
gleaned from our research and ultimately to expedite the continued
upward evolution of women's progress in the workforce.

A shift from women's lack of aspiration for administrative positions to their need for better support systems

An increasing number of women hold certification and degrees
to qualify them for administrative positions (women received 11% of
the doctoral degrees in educational administration in 1972, 20% in
1980, 39% in 1982, and 51% in 1990). Although accurate data on how
many of these women with administrative credentials have actually
sought positions in administration are difficult to obtain, it seems
reasonable to assume that most of them are indeed seeking administrative positions. The importance so frequently relegated to women's
lack of aspiration for executive-level positions as a plausible explanation for their underrepresentation in the field has shifted in recent
years to an increasing emphasis on women's need for better support
systems—role models, mentors, networks, family support—in order
for them to acquire and succeed in executive-level positions (Benton,
1980; Coursen, 1989; Johnson, 1991; Swiderski, 1988).

The culture of educational administration is dominated by white
males and their orientations. Women and minorities have not had
access to networks or sponsors that frequently help males gain entry
into this culture, nor have they had access to on-the-job nurturing
that networks and support systems afford many male administrators, which contribute significantly to their career success and
longevity in a position. Today's research and literature on the topic
indicate a growing regard for career women's need to have stronger
support systems—among themselves as well as the male networks
in order to succeed; furthermore, according to many of today's successful female administrators, the potential for career success seems

greatly enhanced with the help of a mentor(s) (e.g., Garland, 1991; Gupton & Slick, 1994; Lynch, 1990; Myers, 1992; Pavan, 1987). Women, unlike men, traditionally have not benefited from having sponsors or mentors to encourage and support their career advancement.

Ironically, women who aspire to or assume an administrative position are often not even well supported by other women in the profession. Frequently, female administrators report more reluctant acceptance from their female staff members than from male members (Gupton & Slick, 1994). Another problem is that traditionally oriented women often harbor resentment for and even openly defy women who break with tradition and assume positions usually occupied by males (Woo, 1985). Adding insult to injury is the phenomenon known as the "queen bee" syndrome that occurs when a woman in a position of authority works to keep other women out to protect "queenly" status. Schmuck and Schubert also found that "many women who have moved into administrative ranks become inculcated into a culture that supports existing inequitable practices" (Klein & Ortman, 1994, p. 14).

Perhaps because the profession seems appropriately more concerned today about the quality of its leaders rather than with their gender, mentors, networks, and support systems are increasingly targeted as strategic to the nurturance of outstanding leadership for *both* genders. This is especially important for women who have had comparatively little support for career advancement—from male colleagues, from professors of educational administration, from families, from society at large, and from among their own gender within or outside the profession. With the majority of doctoral degrees in educational administration now being awarded to women, to continue to cite women's lack of aspiration as a major contributor to their inequitable representation in administrative positions makes little sense. What is worthwhile, however, is focusing more attention on women's support systems and sponsors, to which positions they are aspiring in educational leadership, and why.

> A shift from women's lack of necessary qualifications and leadership ability to a greater concern about the quality of their preparation and recognition of their leadership talents

With the significant increase in numbers of female graduates in educational administration, the explanation for women's underrepresentation in executive positions in the profession often attributed to their being less qualified than their male counterparts has shifted to a more relevant concern about the *quality* of their preparation and leadership training. The need to incorporate feminine perspectives in knowledge bases and curriculum content in programs of administrator preparation needs to be more openly acknowledged and addressed. Overwhelmingly, university programs perpetuate the exclusion of administrative females to top-ranking positions by relying on curricula based primarily on models of authoritative style leadership (Glazer, 1990). Sociologist Jessie Bernard refers to masculine dominance in organizational studies as the "machismo" factor evidenced by theories and models that

> (1) focus overwhelmingly on the interests and achievements of men; (2) confine women to particular stereotypical areas or define women primarily by their relations to men; (3) focus on men as the subjects of research but unquestioningly generalize their models and findings to women; and (4) value typical male behavioral characteristics more highly than typical female characteristics. (Yeakley, Johnston, & Adkison, 1986, pp. 114-115)

More attention in the literature in the past decade is directed at the need to restructure scholarship and curricula to include the values, needs, and priorities of women's perspectives not dealt with by the dominant organizational theorists to date (Ginn, 1989; Kempner, 1989; Shakeshaft & Nowell, 1984; Styer, 1989). As Klein and Ortman (1994) note, "We need to know how fully women's studies or other aspects of equity based on gender, race, ethnicity, language, disability, social class, and sexual orientation have been integrated into education courses and programs" (p. 16). Just how much restructuring is actually being done by the faculty in higher education is questionable, but the literature at least reflects a shift in its emphasis to focus more accurately on the need for better, more gender-fair preparation of our schools' leaders—both male and female.

Judy Rosener, professor of management at the University of California at Irvine, presented the theory that there is a style of management particular to women in a 1990 article titled "Ways Women Lead" that appeared in the Harvard Business Review. In this article, Dr. Rosener argued that women are more likely than men to manage in an interactive style—encouraging participation, sharing power and information, and enhancing the self-worth of others (Billard, 1992, p. 69). Rosener claimed that women tend to use "transformational" leadership, motivating others by transforming their self-interest into the goals of the organization, while men use "transactional" leadership, doling out rewards for good work and punishment for bad (Billard, 1992, p. 69). In their book *Megatrends for Women*, Aburdene and Naisbitt (1992) refer to the concept of "women's leadership style" and describe it as "open, trusting, compassionate, understanding, and supportive of continuous learning" (McGrew-Zouili, 1993, p. 43). They caution, however, that this style is "not about being nice," but about empowerment, productivity, and outcomes (p. 43).

Reinhartz and King (1993) also caution about the language used to describe leadership attributes of men compared with those of women. The language we use to describe women and men with regard to leadership styles is often not equitable. For example, a man is described as "firm" when dealing with a difficult situation, but under the same conditions, a woman is often referred to as being "stubborn" (p. 9). Language is powerful and conditions the perceptions of people and their roles; in so doing, it may discount the potential of many individuals, specifically women, in leadership roles. With the shifts in ways of thinking about leadership today, perhaps the "softer" language often associated with women and the skills they bring to administrative positions will be better received and less likely to create the barriers described by Reinhartz and King.

Literature about today's reform efforts, for example, frequently references the need for leadership skills usually associated with women; systemic reform emphasizes team-building, interconnectedness, group problem solving, and shared decision making—concepts and skills often associated with female leadership (Anderson, 1993, p. 14). Proponents of systemic reform believe that reform must encompass all aspects of the education system. The kind of leadership needed for this massive reform requires skill in site-based management wherein all the people in the organization are involved. Traditionally, leadership has been consistently characterized by the central values of power and control (Patterson, 1993, p. 2). If necessity is the mother of invention, then perhaps the desperate need for less autocratic leadership in schools across our nation will expedite the movement of more women into positions of authority (Helgesen, 1990; Kempner, 1989; Weller, 1988). Women's more participatory style of leadership should now be more readily accepted—even sought—since greater reliance on and higher regard for transformational leadership skills appear to be fundamental to successful systemic change in today's school reform efforts.

> A shift from focusing solely on too few women acquiring positions in educational administration expanding to include on-the-job maintenance and retention issues

Although gaining equitable access to leadership positions continues to be a major issue for women who aspire to administrative careers in education, job success and retention are relatively new but growing concerns that add further credence to women's need for better support systems throughout their careers.

"Employment discrimination," writes Peitchinis (1989), "refers to access to employment opportunities and to the assignment of responsibilities upon securing of employment" (p. 24). This observation is particularly important in addressing today's issues related to gender equity in the workforce. Peitchinis goes on to say that "the focus must now shift from educational barriers (more women are now prepared academically) . . . to the barriers that make entry into and progression within appropriate employments difficult for women" (p. 24). He further asserts that the worst form of discrimination is underutilizing women's productive capabilities by assigning them to activities beneath their abilities:

> The relative absence of women from the higher echelons of business, government, and institutions will persist as long as women continue to be discriminated against in the allocation of work functions at the lower levels of the hierarchical structure. The critical criterion for accession to high-level positions is work experience and close associations with decision-makers at the higher levels of the structure. Therefore, the nature of work responsibilities undertaken, the committees on which individuals collaborate in their work, the people in the higher echelons to whom individuals report, and the degree of initiative individuals are allowed will all determine the progress up the hierarchical pyramid. (p. 67)

The "glass ceiling" that women often find when they hit middle management and try to move into the upper executive positions is in part due to the expectations for promotion to senior-level positions being quite different from those qualifications necessary at entry- and middle-level management. Peitchinis (1989) explains:

> The qualities for entry into the executive suite are less struc-
> tured and less formal than the qualities required for entry
> into lower-level employments and for rise to middle man-
> agement positions. Breadth of work experience, exposure to
> decision-making under varying conditions and circum-
> stances, and work with senior executives appear to be critical
> qualifications. Women have had limited opportunities to
> acquire such qualifications, which explains the virtual ab-
> sence of women from the executive suite. . . . The positions
> in the organizational structure where work experience rele-
> vant for promotions to the executive suite is gained are
> occupied largely by men, and the required work experience
> is unstructured and undefined. When a requirement is un-
> defined and unstructured it is open to variations to accom-
> modate the experiences of those favoured for elevation.
> (pp. 68-69)

Therefore, once again, the ones in power are at a decided advantage that is not easily challenged by those outside the power loop. This condition makes change slow, if it occurs at all. What Peitchinis recommends and our survey respondents alluded to repeatedly is the need for more objective, productivity-focused criteria to be de-veloped for promotion standards without regard to discriminatory factors such as race or gender. The focus for promotion should be on who can produce the best results—regardless of titles, networks, or who you know. But what *should be* and what *is* are often quite different. Women need to be more aware of what frequently contrib-utes to their stagnation at lower- and middle-level administration and be better prepared to take action by working politically and skillfully to climb the career ladder; once they arrive in the top seat, they should work hard to eliminate such discriminatory practices in the administration of personnel.

The researchers of a study on why women exit the superinten-dency in the field of education observe that "one reason to move beyond deserved concern for entry-level issues is that, with such longstanding, dominant participation of white males in educational leadership, the loss of even a few women and members of underrepresented groups can be significant" (Tallerico, Burstyn, & Poole, 1993, p. 1). This study, commissioned by the National Policy Board for Educational Administration, was based on interviews with 20 women who left their positions as superintendent; the authors found that factors related to their exiting the superintendency were multiple, overlapping, and often cumulative over time. Gender-related problems with the job communicated by the women "ranged from being subtly dissuaded from pursuing the superintendency by professors in university preparation programs, to being blatantly accused of not acting 'tough enough' by board members, administrators, or teachers" (Tallerico et al., 1993, p. 10). The researchers found that additional examples of sex-typed expectations that worked against women superintendents included school boards' perceptions of women's malleability; less remuneration than for males; different interpersonal treatment and more frequent attempts to bully or intimidate women superintendents; closer scrutiny of women's behavior and dress; different and higher performance standards for women; less lateral support for women superintendents among their own ranks; and opportunity for superintendent positions limited to small, rural, or problematic urban districts for the majority of female superintendents. "Essentially," the researchers conclude, "sex-typed expectations work overtly and covertly to make a 'normally' vulnerable leadership role become more so, for its women occupants" (p. 12). Our survey responses and narratives give ample evidence of today's women administrators' vulnerabilities and disadvantages because of their gender in roles typically occupied by men. Communities, boards of education, and the public in general, as well as women themselves, must become more overtly aware of and more skilled at dealing with these discriminatory practices in the workplace that result in what Peitchinis (1989) aptly calls "a significant source of inefficiency in the allocation and use of human resources" (p. 74).

The Ultimate Shift—From Access to Equity

In a recent survey conducted by *Business Week*, half of more than 400 female managers believe that Corporate America is doing "somewhat" better in terms of hiring and promoting women, while half also believe that the rate of progress is slowing ("Corporate Women," 1992, p. 74). More than one third of the respondents thought that in 5 years' time, the number of female senior executives at their companies will have remained the same or fallen ("Corporate Women," 1992, p. 74). Perhaps this is because of the pervasive lack of support within the organization. The "good old boys" network, which has been so helpful for men in moving up the corporate/educational ladder, is largely absent for women (Reinhartz & King, 1993, p. 7). The lack of support, encouragement, and counseling from friends and coworkers as well as superiors makes the executive positions a lonely place for women. For many, this awareness stifles their interest in top-level positions. For those who achieve them, maintaining their leadership status is difficult and discouraging at best. The old saying, "It's lonely at the top," in many instances explains the experience of women in top-level administrative positions. More female executives feel stifled by their companies' male-dominated corporate culture than by a glass ceiling. Whether the isolation of women at the top is intentional or otherwise, it takes its toll.

Although more women in education are achieving the district superintendency (from fewer than 1% in 1980 to sometimes more than 10% in 1990, according to some reports), they are not retaining these positions as long as they once did. Compounding many women administrators' sense of isolation and lack of support is the very real issue of inequitable compensation for positions of equal status with male counterparts. Women administrators' retention rates, their power, as well as their salaries continue to be substantially less than those of male superintendents. "Males still predominate in the higher prestige and higher paid positions at all educational levels of teaching and administration. . . . During the past 20 years there has been a substantial increase in postsecondary educational attainment for women, but this has not been accompanied by similar increases in their income compared to men" (Klein & Ortman, 1994, pp. 14-15). This is partly due to the economic locations where women are hired for their leadership positions.

In our original national survey on women in educational administration conducted in 1993, the majority (73.7%) of the women reporting to be superintendents were in rural school districts. In most instances, the tax base and the revenue generation of rural communities are far less than those of suburban or urban areas. In fact, of the three positions—superintendent, assistant superintendent, and high school principal—rural districts represented the largest (42.9%) overall employer of women in these positions. According to our survey, suburban school districts employ the next largest number of women in the three top-level positions. However, the greatest percentage of the administrative positions held by women in the suburban districts was in the assistant superintendent position. The assistant superintendent position is often seen as the "token" position for women. It is often not the overall power position that requires the major decision making for the district. Only 5.3% of the total number of women responding to our survey held the superintendent's position in the heavily populated urban areas. These positions and those comparable in suburban districts tend to be the most highly paid. Inner-city schools plagued with crime and cultural stress as well as suburban school districts composed typically of well-educated, upper-middle-class Anglos choose male superintendents. These male figures represent stereotypical power and entrepreneurial images of leadership that are generally viewed as preferred in the urban and suburban school districts.

In a different recent national survey conducted by Slick, data were collected regarding Administrators' Perceptions of Clinical Programs in Teacher Preparation. As a part of the survey, which consisted of 1,500 randomly selected elementary, middle school, and high school principals, the respondents were asked, among other things, to identify their positions and gender. Early analysis of these two factors indicates that of the female respondents reporting thus far, all held principalships at the elementary level. Even so, the majority (66%) of elementary principalships were still held by men. Recent national figures report that women make up 43% of elementary principals, 20% of middle school principals, and 11% of high school principals. While accurate figures are difficult to obtain and vary from source to source, women's underrepresentation is a consistency among the data. Gender equity, however, does not rest solely on numbers and sheer titles. When analyzing the progress women are making in educational administration compared with men, focus should be shifted to the more relevant indicators of equity—on-the-job decision-making power and salaries. Equity means for us *equal opportunity and treatment as equals.* The assignment of responsibilities (and thus the power of the position) and the amount of pay should be determined by the skills and efforts of the person, regardless of gender.

With affirmative action programs under fire nationally, the time seems particularly appropriate to reevaluate the status of women and minorities in the workplace. The concept of *evolution* itself suggests an *improving* process, and indeed, the statistical representation of women in educational administration is certainly better than it has been in the past 30 years since the onset of affirmative action (although the improvement has not occurred in a consistently upward profile; there have been setbacks along the way). Evolution also suggests improvement *over time*. Underrepresented groups must naturally master base-level barriers such as becoming properly qualified for competing with the majority group and being willing and having the stamina to take on a host of impediments usually associated with pioneering efforts (i.e., defying role expectations, dealing with self-identity conflicts, having to "prove" oneself capable of the job, receiving more criticism, and scrutiny of job performance). With women's qualifications no longer an issue, and with their increasing numbers in administrative positions, perhaps—as a part of the evolutionary process—women are gaining the experience and seniority without which they have been denied access to many of the administrative positions considered among the most powerful and remunerative. But it must not be assumed that gender equity will unfold naturally in an evolutionary way. Old habits and time-honored gender roles are nebulous and stubbornly resistant to change throughout a society. The two alternative approaches to the problem of job discrimination are using mandates or changing societal attitudes. Obviously, the latter approach is the preferred one. But how do we change attitudes? The most effective way to change attitudes, asserts Peitchinis (1989), is by demonstration (p. 75). And so, we find ourselves back at the gate. If women are routinely denied opportunities to demonstrate their skill and potential, how do they prove themselves capable? Goals and issues pertaining to gender equity will always need to be altered, monitored, and addressed deliberately and strategically until equity is a reality. If this can happen without the heavy hand of Title IX and EEOC laws and affirmative action plans, so much the better. However, history offers little hope that equity will ever be achieved without the mandates in place to keep people from slipping back into familiar patterns of behavior and biased ways of thinking. Mandates are not perfect solutions to the equity issue, but they serve as red flags and reminders needed to curb and ultimately, we hope, to change flawed, unfair practices in a society based on warped, counterproductive—but often accepted as legitimate—attitudes.

10

The Collective Voice: "Go for It!"

Go for it! If administration is what you want, I'm sure women can do as much and just as well as men!

—Jane

Dare to be great!

—The Collective Voice

The overwhelmingly consistent theme of the 150 women administrators, in giving advice to women aspiring to become administrators, was "Go for it!" The implication seemed to be that women needed encouragement and motivation to strive for top-level positions. Women who have achieved their goals of becoming administrators seem to understand that other women might need and want a cheering section to champion their quest for the top. These women expressed repeatedly the persistent belief that everything is possible, just "do it" (Gupton & Slick, 1994).

Unfortunately, many women never seek administrative positions simply because they do not see themselves in positions of leadership. Administration in public education is male dominated and generally accepted as such by both males and females. As a result, quite innocently, it never occurs to many talented women that they should seek positions of leadership. Some of our respondents even admit to the fact that they did not strategically plan their ascent to the top, "it just happened." Apparently, once at the top, they reflected upon how they reached their positions and began to realize the actions they had taken that made their ascent possible. These women made the following statements to encourage others:

> Remember it's up to you—decide what you want and then strive for it.

> Be willing to take risks.

> Be open to new opportunities, challenges and experiences.

> Dare to be different.

> If you stumble or fall on hard times, pick yourself up and carry on—don't give up.

There is another side of the coin when it comes to women seeking administrative positions. Even though our respondents overwhelmingly indicated that an aspiring female administrator should "go for it," if her assertiveness is seen as being too aggressive, she can defeat herself before she gets very far along in the process. Emily laid it on the line: "A woman who demonstrates the same aggressiveness [as a man] is called a bitch or a pushy broad. I still see the hesitation to accept in women "go-getter" qualities." Consequently, the "go for it" attitude is a plus for women seeking administrative positions as long as it is not seen as *too* aggressive. It is a fine line to have to walk, and definitely, the particulars of the district situation will affect the readiness of others in the system and in the community for a woman administrator with initiative to be accepted.

Jane's story was one of the most interesting and unique stories shared with us. She had spent many years in a local school district as teacher, administrator, and superintendent during a time, historically, when women rarely aspired or achieved leadership in public school education. Yet because of her close connections with the community and deep respect of the many students she had taught, she was entrusted more and more with key decision-making responsibilities and positions of authority. She was not one of our women who actually sought leadership positions; rather, she grew into them. However, in her own words, as she reflects upon her professional experiences, Jane says:

I haven't touched on why I wasn't promoted—I really didn't ask for it. I liked teaching and I thought I was important. Men just seemed to get it! It would have meant higher wages and a higher pension now. I have no regrets; I loved teaching. I should have been more aggressive perhaps.

Advice—Go for it!—if administration is what you want. I'm sure women can do as much and just as well as men!

After 66 years in the profession, Jane appears to be taking an honest look at what she has been able to achieve and perhaps realizing that she could have reached her administrative positions earlier in her career had she made the conscious effort to do so. Above all, however, she expressed a pride in always caring about those with whom she was working, thereby maintaining her integrity regarding what was really important in the profession—developing children's love for learning and carefully, lovingly giving all students the sense of being special.

In the original survey, which was sent to 300 current administrators in the profession, the final section of the survey asked the respondents to share their best advice for women aspiring to positions of administration in the profession. One astute respondent, about to be installed as the first elected female State Superintendent of Public Instruction in her state, gave the following advice specifically related to "going for it":

List pros and cons of "going for it," and make sure that it is what you want. Go for it! Be prepared to work harder than you've ever worked!

She is encouraging others to "go for it," but reminds them realistically that they will really have to work for what they achieve.

Often, the spirited advice given by our respondents comes close to sounding like a cheering team trying to get the aspiring female administrators to believe in themselves and the dreams they have of becoming leaders. It was a heartening experience to read of the respondents' willingness to share their experiences and words of encouragement. "Just do it" was also a common bit of advice that these women gave. They also advised, "Do not take a position that is not what you really want." In other words, go for what you want;

don't sacrifice your goal for something less. Once again, it sounds like our respondents felt a need to bolster the self-esteem of aspiring female administrators so that they would believe in themselves and what they want to achieve. "Never give up" was also frequently given as advice. "You can do it" was another statement the respondents shared often. One respondent said, "My dad always told me, 'You can be anything you want as long as you are willing to work hard.'" Others offered the following statements:

> Keep pushing for the position you would like to have. (County superintendent of schools)

> If you want it . . . go for it! (Superintendent of schools)

> Women care and want the best, and I encourage women to roll up their sleeves and go for it! (High school principal)

> Ignore the reasons why you cannot become an administrator, and concentrate on all of the reasons why you would be effective. (High school principal)

> Go for it and help each other. Change the attitudes of our bosses (and husbands) through our concerted efforts and persistence. (High school principal)

> Don't sell yourself short. You can do it. (Assistant superintendent)

> If you want to do it—DO IT! (Principal)

> Just do it. How does one have the courage . . . the resolve . . . the determination . . . the resiliency . . . the audacity . . .? Just do it! (Principal)

> Set a goal—go for it! (Assistant superintendent)

> Believe in your ability to succeed! (Principal)

> Don't ever give up! (Administrative assistant)

Remember it's up to you—decide what you want and then strive for it! (Assistant superintendent)

You can do whatever your inner desires want. There are no barriers unless you make them! (Superintendent)

Prepare yourself with the appropriate credentials, then keep striving to obtain a job. Do not give up, but keep pressing on. (Principal)

Go for it—but be sure you have happily balanced or clarified work and family priorities. (Principal)

And finally, from the original survey, a respondent summarizes the spirit of encouragement that so many expressed:

I also say "go for it." It's a great challenge and there is the satisfaction of knowing that you have achieved something your female peers will never achieve. Dare to be different, dare to be Great! (High school principal)

We think it would be safe to say that our women respondents have a lot of spunk, courage, and persistent belief that eventually they will succeed in reaching their goal of becoming administrators. From all of the advice that they give, it also appears that this persistent belief in the self and the "go for it" attitude played a tremendous part in their overall success in achieving their positions. Once again, the cheering spirit of belief that the next-to-impossible can be accomplished is expressed in Denise's comments below:

Maybe I should have a T-shirt made with either "It's Never Too Late!" or "Nothing's Impossible" written on it. But perhaps, our school's slogan of "Aim for Success" would be best.

Catherine shares her advice, which touches on an aspect that can thwart a woman's own professional dreams—sublimating one's career for that of another. She states:

First, my best advice is to pursue your own dreams—don't sacrifice for someone else. You never know what the future holds. I missed my own chance at a college experience—not just the degree, but the excitement of discovering myself, instead of becoming an instant provider/caretaker to ensure someone else's success.

There is always the danger of never fulfilling one's own potential and professional goals if one postpones too long. We believe that our respondents would have aspiring female administrators carefully weigh their professional goals in light of their personal responsibilities, and then strive to do what is both best and prudent in a timely manner. They would also, we believe, encourage a woman with leadership potential not to allow her opportunity to pass her by. GO FOR IT! means exactly what it states: Pursue your goals with courage, confidence, and full awareness of and preparation for the many challenges you will encounter and be able to overcome!

Call to Action

Over the past decade, the literature regarding women in educational administration has increasingly focused on what needs to happen to improve the quality of leadership in education for everyone irrespective of gender. However, until all human potential is given equal access to leadership positions, the discriminatory, exclusionary practices of selecting educational administrators will continue to stifle the integrity of the profession and make a mockery of the educational process. In the following quote, Charol Shakeshaft (1986b), leading researcher and authority in the field of educational administration, eloquently and succinctly focuses on the real issues at stake:

> What is important is what being a female and being a male means for interacting as workers, for making moral and ethical decisions, for understanding different points of view, for the way one balances one's time, or for what one sees as important tasks for an administrator. All of these and more are influenced by gender. We need to understand what gender means for effective school administration. (p. 216)

The challenge for all administrators, present and future, is *to take action* to address these issues proactively. Strategies to overcome discrimination in order for the pool of leadership talent to be inclusive of all people must ensure equal access for both genders, but more than this, they must ultimately result in equitable hiring and treatment of both genders in the workplace. By equal hiring and treatment in the workplace, we mean that all persons with the qualifications and skills for administrative positions should be treated similarly in hiring and promotion practices. This does not necessarily mean that the percentage of women administrators will match the percentage of women teachers in education; nor does equity for us mean a 50-50 split between men and women in administration. Rather, real equity means that the hiring and treatment of employees are based on *qualifications, skills,* and *performance.* Personnel practices that result in the exclusionary treatment of any group of people as a function of their race, doctrine, or gender are not appropriate, just, or organizationally efficacious. Recommendations for achieving equity in educational administration have individual, organizational, and societal dimensions. The individual's call to action requires that people take responsibility for ensuring better treatment of women in educational administration; the political, organizational, and societal dimensions pertain to action that must take place at broader levels to move from policy to practice, from rhetoric to reality, and from access to true equitable treatment of both genders in the workplace:

Recommendations for the Individual Person

1. Women and men must believe in women's ability to be leaders.
2. Women must believe that positions of leadership are indeed attainable for them.
3. Women must not be daunted by the small number of women in positions of leadership.
4. Women must treat their own gender better in the workplace.
5. Men must nurture the leadership potential of women as well as men.
6. Women and men must mentor and sponsor women as well as men for leadership in the profession.
7. Women must not feel that their femininity and identity in the social order are violated by assuming leadership roles.

8. Women and men must learn to move beyond toleration to full-fledged appreciation of the differences in male and female perspectives within the organization.

9. Women must become more politically aware and active at all levels—locally, statewide, nationally.

10. Women must actively plan their careers and chart a course of specific strategies—and help their daughters to do the same!

11. Women should seek people in personal relationships—husbands, friends, and significant others—who support their career goals.

12. Women should seek to develop and become part of networks of support at all levels for personal as well as professional growth and nurturing of self and others.

Recommendations for Political and Social Systems and Organizations

1. School districts must move from writing good policy to practicing fairer treatment of women in seeking and attaining administrative positions in education.

2. School board members should broaden their perceptual image of school leaders.

3. Communities must view male and female leadership potential and ability equally.

4. Communities must nurture politically and financially the preparation of women for leadership.

5. State departments must set a precedent of modeling nondiscriminatory policy making and personnel practices that demonstrate inclusivity.

6. State legislatures must provide funding and support to local school districts for nurturing the inclusivity of underrepresented groups of people in leadership positions.

7. The federal government should provide more adequate funding for research and development of projects and programs related to the advancement of women in educational administration.

8. Higher education must provide better programs of training and education that are expanded to include the female as well as the male perspective regarding organizational theory and practice.

9. Higher education faculties must recruit more female professors of educational administration and should actively seek to promote more females into positions of leadership (e.g., department chairpersons and deans).

10. Professional organizations need to promote a persona of leadership in the profession that focuses on ability, preparation, experience, and/or potential, rather than gender.

Trying to decide where change should initiate can be stagnating and counterproductive. Must women and men as individuals do more introspective analyses of the problems they often create for themselves and others because of the issue of gender in the workplace? Or must school administrators, state departments, school board and community members, professional organizations, institutions of higher learning, and governmental agencies at all levels take charge of more assertive action to ensure that the leadership potential of all educators is equitably tapped? The answer is *yes* and *yes*; simultaneous efforts from all dimensions to deal with the pervasive problems of discrimination in the profession are essential. Individual women may seek advice and mentors and may take preparatory action that readies them for administrative positions; but until the social systems they are attempting to enter are accepting of them, the individual will not have much success and may become even more frustrated with the existing external barriers. The recommendations offered above are intended to be comprehensive and inclusive of all individuals as well as the organizational and political aspects that affect the issue of underrepresentation of women in educational administration. The challenge for all educators—indeed, for our society—is to appreciate and encourage the strengths of men and women who have the commitment and dedication to seek positions of educational leadership that are so desperately needed to nurture and guide the young people of this nation.

References

Aburdene, P., & Naisbitt, J. (1992). *Megatrends for women*. New York: Villard.

Anderson, B. (1993). The stages of systematic change. *Educational Leadership, 51*(1), 14-17.

Andrews, R. L., & Basom, M. R. (1990). Instructional leadership: Are women principals better? *Principal, 70*(2), 38-40.

Benton, S. Y. (1980). Women administrators for the 1980's: A new breed. *Journal of the National Association of Women Deans, Administrators, and Counselors, 43*(4), 18-23.

Beyer-Houda, B., & Ruhl-Smith, C. (1995). Leadership styles of school administrators in the panhandle of Texas: A comparative study. In B. J. Irby & G. Brown (Eds.), *Women as school executives: Voices and visions* (pp. 42-44). Huntsville: Sam Houston Press and Texas Council of Women School Executives.

Biklen, S. K., & Brannigan, M. (1980). *Women and educational leadership*. Lexington, MA: D. C. Heath.

Billard, M. (1992). Do women make better managers? *Working Woman, 3*, 68-73.

Blount, J. M. (1993, April). *The genderization of the superintendency: A statistical portrait*. Paper presented at the annual meeting of the American Educational Research Association, Atlanta, GA.

Bonuso, C., & Shakeshaft, C. (1983). The gender of secondary school principals. *Integrated Education, 21*(6), 143-146.

Brooks, G. H., & Regan, H. B. (1995). *Out of women's experience: Creating relational leadership.* Thousand Oaks, CA: Corwin.

Brown, D. J. (1981). The financial penalty of the sex talent inversion in Canadian education. *Interchange, 12*(1), 69-82.

Brown, G., & Merchant, J. (1993). Women in leadership: A support system for success. In G. Brown & B. Irby (Eds.), *Women as school executives: A powerful paradigm* (pp. 87-92). Huntsville: Sam Houston Press and Texas Council of Women School Executives..

Corporate women. (1992, June 8). *Business Week,* pp. 76-78.

Coursen, D. (1989). *Two special cases: Women and blacks.* Eugene, OR: ERIC Clearinghouse on Educational Management. (ERIC Document Reproduction Service No. ED 309 508)

Criswell, M., & Betz, L. (1995). Attitudes toward women administrators among school board members: A current perspective. In B. J. Irby & G. Brown (Eds.), *Women as school executives: Voices and visions* (pp. 28-34). Huntsville: Sam Houston Press and Texas Council of Women School Executives.

Fields, C. (1995, November 17-19). Families and values. *USA Weekend,* pp. 4, 5, 6, 8-10.

Funk, C. (1995). Women as school executives: The winter and the warm. In B. J. Irby & G. Brown (Eds.), *Women as school executives: Voices and visions* (pp. 64-70). Huntsville: Sam Houston Press and Texas Council of Women School Executives.

Gallese, L. R. (1991). Why women aren't making it to the top. *Across the Board, 28*(4), 18-22.

Garland, S. B. (1991, September 2). How to keep women managers on the corporate ladder. *Business Week,* p. 64.

Ginn, L. W. (1989). A quick look at the past, present, and future of women in public school administration. *Research in Education.* (RIE Document Reproduction No. ED 310 498)

Glazer, J. S. (1990). *Feminism and professionalism: The case of education and business.* Paper presented at the annual meeting of the Association for the Study of Higher Education. (ERIC Document Reproduction No. ED 326 120)

Gotwalt, N., & Towns, K. (1986). Rare as they are women at the top can teach us all. *The Executive Educator, 12,* 13-29.

Green, M. F. (1982). A Washington perspective on women and networking: The power & the pitfalls. *Journal of the National Association for Women Deans, Administrators, and Counselors, 46*(1), 65-83.

Gupton, S. L., & Slick, G. A. (1994). The missing pieces in emerging female leadership in the profession: Support systems, mentoring, and networking. *Mississippi Educational Leadership, 1*(1), 13-18.

Helgesen, S. (1990). *The female advantage: Women's ways of leadership.* New York: Doubleday.

Hennig, M., & Jardim, A. (1977). *The managerial woman.* New York: Doubleday.

Hill, M. S., & Ragland, J. C. (1995). *Women as educational leaders.* Thousand Oaks, CA: Corwin.

Holzman, M. (1993). What is systematic change? *Educational Leadership, 51*(1), 18.

Johnson, J. R. (1991). Networking: How to permeate the glass ceiling—Some highlights from recent studies of networking among women. *Research in Education.* (RIE Document Reproduction No. ED 332 356)

Kanter, R. (1983). *The change masters: Innovations for productivity in the American corporation.* New York: Simon & Schuster.

Kempner, K. (1989). Getting into the castle of educational administration. *Peabody Journal of Education, 66*(3), 104-123.

Klein, S. S., & Ortman, P. E. (1994). Continuing the journey toward gender equity. *Educational Researcher, 23*(8), 13-21.

Kram, K. (1983). Phases of the mentor relationship. *Academy of Management Journal, 26*(4), 608-625.

Lambert, P. (1989). Women into educational management. *Adults Learning, 1*(4), 106-107.

Langford, T. (1995). The feminine agenda: Transformational and creative leadership. In B. J. Irby & G. Brown (Eds.), *Women as school executives: Voices and visions* (pp. 99-106). Huntsville: Sam Houston Press and Texas Council of Women School Executives.

Levinson, D., et al. (1978). *The seasons of a man's life.* New York: Knopf.

Lunenburg, F., & Ornstein, A. C. (1991). *Educational administration.* Belmont, CA: Wadsworth.

Lynch, K. K. (1990, August). Women in school administration: Overcoming the barriers to advancement. *Women's Educational Equity Act Publishing Center Digest,* p. 2.

McGrath, S. T. (1992). Here come the women! *Educational Leadership, 49*(5), 62-65.

McGrew-Zouli, R. (1993). Women's leadership style. In G. Brown & B. Irby (Eds.), *Women as school executives: A powerful paradigm* (pp. 43-45). Huntsville: Sam Houston Press and Texas Council for Women School Executives.

McMillan, T. (1995, December 15-17). The trouble with women. *USA Weekend*, pp. 4-5.

Mellow, G. O. (1988). Women's centers and women administrators: Breaking the glass slipper together. *Initiatives, 51*(2-3), 53-58.

Moir, A., & Jessel, D. (1992). *Brain sex.* New York: Dell.

Myers, W. S. (1992). How to find the perfect mentor. *Women in Business, 3,* 22-23.

Naisbitt, J., & Aburdene, P. (1990). *Megatrends 2000: Ten new directions for the 1990's.* New York: Morrow.

Newman, S. G. (1978). Role conflicts of a female academic. *Intellect, 2,* 302-306.

Norris, C. J. (1994). Cultivating creative cultures. In L. H. Hughes (Ed.), *The principal as leader* (pp. 61-79). New York: Macmillan.

Ortiz, F. I., & Marshall, C. (1988). Women in educational administration. In N. J. Bogan (Ed.), *Handbook of research on educational administration* (pp. 123-141). New York: Longman.

Patterson, J. (1993). *Leadership for tomorrow's schools.* Alexandria, VA: Association of Supervision and Curriculum Development.

Pavan, B. N. (1987). Mentoring certified aspiring and incumbent female and male public school administrators. *Journal of Educational Equity and Leadership, 7*(4), 318-331.

Pavan, B. N. (1989). Searching for female leaders for America's schools: Are the women to blame? *Research in Education.* (RIE Document Reproduction No. ED 332 356)

Peitchinis, Stephen G. (1989). *Women at work: Discrimination and response.* Toronto, Ontario: McClelland & Stewart.

Phillips, L. (1978). Mentors and proteges: A study of the career development of women managers and executives in business and industry (Doctoral dissertation, University of California at Los Angeles). *Dissertation Abstracts International, 38*(11), 6414A.

Quality Education Data. (1992, October). *Personnel selections: Gender.* Denver.

Reinhartz, J., & King, F. L. (1993). Clarifying the paradigm: Women in leadership positions. In G. Brown & B. J. Irby (Eds.), *Women as school executives: A powerful paradigm* (pp. 7-12). Huntsville: Sam Houston Press and Texas Council of Women School Executives.

Rist, M. C. (1991). Opening your own doors. *The Executive Educator, 13*(1), 14.

Rogers, M., & Davis, J. (1991). Women of substance. *Research in Education*. (RIE Document Reproduction No. ED 331 155)

Scandura, T. A. (1990). *Breaking the glass ceiling in the 1990's*. Research project funded by the U.S. Dept. of Labor, Women's Bureau.

Schmuck, P. A. (1986). Networking: A new word, a different game. *Educational Leadership, 43*(5), 60-61.

Shakeshaft, C. (1986a). A gender at risk. *Phi Delta Kappan, 67*(7), 499-503.

Shakeshaft, C. (1986b). *Women in educational administration*. Beverly Hills, CA: Sage.

Shakeshaft, C., & Nowell, I. (1984). Research on theories, concepts, and models of organizational behavior: The influence of gender. *Issues in Education, 2*, 186-203.

Short, P. M. & others. (1989). Women professors of educational administration: A profile and salient issues. *Research in Education*. (RIE Document Reproduction No. ED 306 656)

Slick, G. A., & Gupton, S. L. (1993). Voices of experience: Best advice to prospective and practicing women administrators from education's top female executives. In G. Brown & B. J. Irby (Eds.), *Women as school executives: A powerful paradigm* (pp. 75-85). Huntsville: Sam Houston Press and Texas Council of Women School Executives.

Styer, S. (1989). Addressing women's issues in educational administration preparation programs. *Research in Education*. (RIE Document Reproduction No. ED 312 738)

Swiderski, W. (1988). Problems faced by women in gaining access to administrative positions in education. *Education Canada, 28*(3), 24-31.

Tallerico, M., Burstyn, J. N., & Poole, W. (1993). *Gender and politics at work: Why women exit the superintendency*. Fairfax, VA: The National Policy Board for Educational Administration.

Thomas, M. D. (1986). Why aren't women administering our schools? *NASSP Bulletin, 70*(488), 90-92.

Tibbetts, S. L. (1980). The woman principal: Superior to the male? *Journal of the National Association for Women Deans, Administrators, and Counselors, 43*(4), 15-18.

Tyree, C. (1995). Women in education: Are we perpetuating societal attitudes by moving toward an androgynous leadership style? In B. J. Irby & G. Brown (Eds.), *Women as school executives: Voices and visions* (pp. 22-25). Huntsville: Sam Houston Press and Texas Council of Women School Executives.

Weber, M., Feldman, J. R., & Poling, E. C. (1981). Why women are underrepresented in educational administration. *Educational Leadership, 38*(4), 320-322.

Welch, O. M. (1993, May). *Mentoring in educational settings.* Newton, MA: Women's Educational Equity Act Publishing Center.

Weller, J. (1988). *Women in educational leadership* [Monograph 3(4)]. Columbus: Ohio State University, Center for Sex Equity, Ohio State Department of Education, Division of Vocational Education.

Wesson, L. H. (1995). Women and minorities in education administration. In B. J. Irby & G. Brown (Eds.), *Women as school executives: Voices and visions* (pp. 149-158). Huntsville: Sam Houston Press and Texas Council of Women School Executives.

Whitecraft, C., & Williams, M. L. (1990). Gender difference and public sector managers: Women's perceptions of equality in state government. *Research in Education.* (RIE Document Reproduction No. ED 324 435)

Woo, L. (1985). Women administrators: Profiles of success. *Phi Delta Kappan, 67*(4), 285-288.

Yeakley, C. C., Johnston, G. S., & Adkison, J. A. (1986). In pursuit of equity: A review of research on minorities and women in educational administration. *Educational Administration Quarterly, 22*(3), 110-149.

York, R. O. & others. (1988). The power of positive mentors: Variables associated with women's interest in social work administration. *Journal of Social Work Education, 24*(3), 242-250.

Appendix A

Education's Women Administrators

Their Paths To The Top

Research Conducted by
Gloria Slick, Ed.D. and
Sandra Gupton, Ed.D.
Copyright, 1993
The University of Southern Mississippi

Women In Education Questionnaire

I. Beliefs About Women's Issues in the Workplace

This section is concerned with the issues affecting the number of women in top-level administrative positions in education. Indicate whether you agree or disagree with each statement and to what extent by circling the appropriate indicator.

SA	-	Strongly Agree
A	-	Agree
U	-	Undecided
D	-	Disagree
SD	-	Strongly Disagree

1. Many women are seeking administrative positions in education.   SA   A   U   D   SD

2. Women are supportive of other women in the profession.   SA   A   U   D   SD

3. Women are perceived to be as powerful on the job as men.   SA   A   U   D   SD

4. Women are more sensitive to people matters than men.   SA   A   U   D   SD

5. Women are more concerned about process than the end result.   SA   A   U   D   SD

6. Women are not as effective in their decision-making as men.   SA   A   U   D   SD

7. Women are incapable of financial finesse.   SA   A   U   D   SD

8. Women lack delegation skills.   SA   A   U   D   SD

9. Career women are frequently torn between family and work responsibilities.   SA   A   U   D   SD

10. Women often lack freedom of geographic mobility which impedes their career advancement.   SA   A   U   D   SD

11. Women are frequently perceived in stereotyped roles.   SA   A   U   D   SD

12. Women lack political savvy.   SA   A   U   D   SD

(CONT'D)

2.

I. Beliefs About Women's Issues in the Workplace (cont'd)

13. Women work harder than men for less money.   SA A U D SD

14. Many women receive token placement at the assistant
    superintendent level.   SA A U D SD

15. Women are more capable than men at managing team
    (collaborative) work efforts.   SA A U D SD

16. Women in administration are more people-oriented than
    men in administration.   SA A U D SD

17. Women are not good mediators.   SA A U D SD

18. Women are good manipulators of people and the tasks
    that need to be completed.   SA A U D SD

19. The "good 'old boy" system is alive and well in educational
    administration.   SA A U D SD

20. Women are good organizers and can keep focused on
    what needs to be accomplished.   SA A U D SD

21. Women are more dedicated to the education of children
    than in doing what is politically advantageous.   SA A U D SD

22. Women value personal relationships more than power.   SA A U D SD

23. Women are more interested in process than pecking order.   SA A U D SD

24. Innate gender differences account primarily for the ways
    men and women function on the job.   SA A U D SD

25. No amount of training or acculturation will make the
    genders think or administer alike.   SA A U D SD

II. Career Paths   3.

A.   **Career Motives and Beliefs**: Another important area of research deals with tracing women's paths to the top. Please respond to each of the following questions by circling one response or filling in the blank that best describes your personal experiences or perceptions.

1.   When did you decide to become an administrator?
     a.   As a child
     b.   As an undergraduate student
     c.   After several years as a teacher
     d.   After my children were grown
     e.   Other_____

2.   What is the primary reason you decided to become an administrator?
     a.   For career challenge and satisfaction
     b.   For improved salary
     c.   To make positive changes in education for young people
     d.   Encouragement from others
     e.   Other _____

3.   How long did it take you to get an advanced degree or certificate to be qualified as an administrator?_____year(s)

4.   Did you continue to work as you pursued the advanced degree?
     a.   Yes - worked fulltime
     b.   No - did not work
     c.   Worked part-time

5.   After you earned the necessary credentials, how long did it take you to get an administrative position?_____/_____months/years

6.   Did you get promoted to your first administrative position within the system in which you were currently employed at the time?
     a.   Yes - promoted within
     b.   No - Obtained position within the state
     c.   No - Obtained position out of state

7.   How old were you when you got your first administrative position?
     _____years

8.   Have you ever assumed an administrative position that had never been held by a female?_____ What was the position?_____

4.

B. Professional Career Experiences: In order to have a complete picture of your career path to the top, it is important for a record of your professional experiences to be given. Please fill in the requested information in the concise format provided below. Begin with your first position after graduation from college and list each subsequent position up to your current job:

1.

Type of Position	Name of School District/ Location (State)	How Long?	Why Left?
a. _____	_____	_____	_____
b. _____	_____	_____	_____
c. _____	_____	_____	_____
d. _____	_____	_____	_____

2. Current Position:

a. Title:_____

b. Type of District (check one) _____Rural; _____Urban; _____Suburban;

_____Other

d. District Enrollment #: _____

e. Why do you think you were hired for this position? Check all responses that apply.

_____ Token female
_____ Potential leadership qualities
_____ Affirmative action compliance
_____ Longevity
_____ Best qualified for position in terms of experience
_____ Best qualified for position in terms of formal preparation
_____ Reward for loyalty
_____ Next step in upward mobility (of positions)
_____ Reward for hard work
_____ Expert in community relations/good mediator
_____ Effective manager
Other:_____

5.

C. **Career-related barriers**: In the evolution of your career, you may have encountered several obstacles in attaining your goals. With this in mind, please list or describe the major barriers you experienced in each of the following steps of your career.

1. Choosing a major area of study or career.

2. Obtaining the necessary degree or training.

3. Securing a job after college. (The first job in the profession)

4. Advancing in your career.

5. Balancing family and career.

6. Encountering barriers that were gender-related.

6.

D. Career Assessment: As you advanced your career you may have reflected on the costs and trials of traveling the path to the top. In this section, please respond by indicating whether you agree or disagree with each statement and to what extent by circling the appropriate indicator.

SA = Strongly Agree
A = Agree
U = Undecided
D = Disagree
SD = Strongly Disagree

1. I would pursue my career if I had it to do all over again.   SA   A   U   D   SD

2. I feel I have had to make substantial personal sacrifices to advance my career.   SA   A   U   D   SD

3. For the most part, I believe claims by women concerning gender discrimination in educational administration are justified.   SA   A   U   D   SD

4. I feel alienated or psychologically separated from the rest of the immediate work group as a result of my executive status.   SA   A   U   D   SD

5. I feel that affirmative action laws have helped to open doors for career advancement for me as a woman.   SA   A   U   D   SD

6. I feel my femininity has been diminished as a result of my career as an executive.   SA   A   U   D   SD

7. I affiliate more with men than women on the job.   SA   A   U   D   SD

8. I am comfortable with my level of power in the organization.   SA   A   U   D   SD

9. I feel my subordinates are comfortable with my power in the organization.   SA   A   U   D   SD

10. I feel my physical attractiveness has positively affected my career advancement.   SA   A   U   D   SD

7.

III. Significant Life Influences Affecting Your Career:

A. Positive Role Models: (One whom you admired and tried to emulate, but may not have known personally.) List the person(s) who served as positive role model(s) for you as you progressed in your career. Indicate, the gender, age and primary features of each role model. Also, indicate your age at the time. This person may have been a friend, a relative or a professional educator.

Person (s)	Gender	Age of role model	Your Age	Characteristics/ Behaviors/Admired
Ex.: 5th grade teacher	Female	40's	10	Goal-Oriented, Nurturing

1. _____

2. _____

B. Negative Role Models: (One whose characteristics or behaviors you have tried to avoid.) Please follow the same instructions as above

Person (s)	Gender	Age of role model	Your Age	Characteristics/ Behaviors/Avoided

1. _____

2. _____

C. Mentors: (One with whom you formed a professional interpersonal relationship and who provided beneficial career and psychosocial support to you.)

1. If you have had a mentor who fits this definition, indicate below the person's position, gender, and age at the time of the mentoring relationship. Using the example provided below as a guide, complete the additional information requested.

Person	Gender	Their Age	Your Age	How Relationship Established	Length of Relationship	Current Status of Relationship	Mentor's Characteristics
Ex. Professor	M	42	25	Graduate Asst.	Ongoing	Collegial	Caring, Supportive

a._____

b._____

If you listed a mentor(s) in C-1., please complete part C-2. of the questionnaire. Otherwise, proceed to part III D.

8.

2. Mentoring Behaviors: This section is designed to determine what types of supportive behaviors were most manifested by your mentor(s). Circle the response which best represents the degree to which your mentor exhibited the following behaviors.

AA = Almost Always
F = Frequently
ST = Sometimes
S = Seldom
AN = Almost Never

BEHAVIORS

a.	Teaching	AA	F	ST	S	AN
b.	Guiding	AA	F	ST	S	AN
c.	Advising and counseling	AA	F	ST	S	AN
d.	Sponsoring (opening doors, providing opportunities)	AA	F	ST	S	AN
e.	Role-modeling (exemplar)	AA	F	ST	S	AN
f.	Validating (reassuring)	AA	F	ST	S	AN
g.	Motivating (encouraging growth and risk-taking)	AA	F	ST	S	AN
h.	Protecting (defending, admonishing, buffering)	AA	F	ST	S	AN
i.	Communicating (responding, listening, informing)	AA	F	ST	S	AN
j.	Being subtle and not expecting credit (quietly supportive)	AA	F	ST	S	AN
k.	Other_____ _____					

D. Have you ever been a mentor to someone in the profession?
   1.   Yes
   2.   No

E. Are you a part of a strong network of supportive women in the profession?
   1.   Yes
   2.   No, don't see a need for it.
   3.   No, but would like to be.

F. Please describe any additiional influences that you feel significantly contributed to your career attainment. Briefly explain how.

9.

IV. Leadership Characteristics

A. Compared to your **male counterparts in similar positions**, do you feel that you are MORE, SAME, or LESS as they in each of the following attributes? Circle your chosen response:

1.	Aggressive	More	Less	Same
2.	Competitive	More	Less	Same
3.	Verbally oriented	More	Less	Same
4.	Spatially oriented	More	Less	Same
5.	Cooperative	More	Less	Same
6.	Motivated by power	More	Less	Same
7.	Concerned about personal relationships	More	Less	Same
8.	Career oriented	More	Less	Same
9.	Family oriented	More	Less	Same
10.	Androgynous	More	Less	Same

B. Compared to other **females in general**, do you feel that you are MORE, SAME, or LESS as they in each of these attributes? Circle your chosen response.

1.	Aggressive	More	Less	Same
2.	Competitive	More	Less	Same
3.	Verbally oriented	More	Less	Same
4.	Spatially oriented	More	Less	Same
5.	Cooperative	More	Less	Same
6.	Motivated by power	More	Less	Same
7.	Concerned about personal relationships	More	Less	Same
8.	Career oriented	More	Less	Same
9.	Family oriented	More	Less	Same
10.	Androgynous	More	Less	Same

C. Please comment briefly on whether you believe women have as much leadership potential as men:_____

_____

_____

_____

V. Demographics   10.

The information requested below will assist us in ascertaining data that are highly pertinent to the overall questionnaire.   Please fill in the blank or circle the letter of your response to each of the following questions. Thank you for your assistance in this area.

A. Personal Data

1.   Age_____   Weight _____   Height _____
2.   Place of Birth_____
                           city   state
3.   Race_____ Ethnic Orgin_____
4.   Health Status   a. Good   b. Fair   c. Poor
5.   Health concerns/problems_____

_____

6.   Healthful Living Activites. Circle all of those you practice on a regular basis.
     a.   Nutrition   b. Exercise   c. Recreation   d. Relaxation
7.   Marital Status: (circle the appropriate response)
     a. Married   b. Single   c. Divorced   d. Widowed
8.   Number of times married _____ Number of times divorced_____
9.   Children:_____   Ages: _____
10. Are you left-handed or right-handed? _____

B. Community Affiliations (current)

1.   Community type: Circle the word that best describes the type of community in
     which you live.   a. rural   b. urban   c. suburban
2.   Religious affiliation: _____
3.   Civic organizations: _____
4.   Political affiliation: _____
5.   Professional affiliation(s) ex: ATE, IRA, etc. _____

_____

C.Family and Relationships   11.
    1.   Spouse (fill in blank)
        a.   Current job_____ _ __
        b.   Level of education_____

    2.   Your parents (fill in blank)
        a.   Mother's occupation_____
            Level of education_____
        b.   Father's occupation_____
            Level of education_____

    3.   Your home environment as a child (circle appropriate response)
        a.   Two parent
        b.   Single parent
        c.   Other_____

    4.   Your siblings (fill in blank)
        a.   No. of children in family_____
        b.   No. of brothers_____
        c.   No. of sisters_____
        d.   Your position in the family: (circle appropriate response)
            1. Oldest
            2. Middle
            3. Youngest
            4. Only child

Please Consider: We realize that through personal interaction, valuable information could surface in relation to the issues addressed in this questionnaire. Therefore we are suggesting the possibility of personal inteviews. Please respond to the following query.

  A.   Would you be interested in being interviewed concerning the issues presented in this questionnaire? If so, please indicate your preference in facilitating a possible interview by circling the appropriate number.

    1.   Telephone interview - Phone #_(_____)_____
    2.   Interview session during the Association of Teacher Educators (ATE) Conference in Los Angeles (Feb. 11-14, 1993)
    3.   Other _____

VI. Final Comments 12.

A. The following is a list of the more frequent explanations for women's lack of equitable representation in educational administration. Please react by prioritizing them in rank order from #1 (most important reason) to #5 (least important reason).

_____ a. Women's lack of aspiration to top level administrative posts.
_____ b. Innate, biologically programmed differences in how the sexes
think, what they value, and how they function.
_____ c. Cultural stereotyping of "appropriate roles" for men and women.
_____ d. Insufficient role-modeling, networking, and mentoring among women.
_____ e. Inadequate training and educational opportunity.

B. Please share your best advice to other women aspiring to positions similiar to yours.

VII. Optional Information   13.

The information requested below is important to the overall survey, but your participation is optional. As we mentioned earlier, all the information you share with us through this questionnaire will remain confidential. If you choose to complete this part of the survey, it will allow us to continue the research by doing a longitudinal survey at some later date as well as provide us the opportunity to send you the results of this initial research. Thank you for your consideration in this matter.

A.   Name_____
                        last   first   middle initial

B.   Address (current home)_____
                                              street address

     _____
              city   state   zip

C.   Address (current office)_____
                                              street address

     _____
              city   state   zip

D.   Phone Numbers (____)_____ (____)_____
                                    office   home

We sincerely thank you for your time and effort to complete this questionnaire in a candid and timely manner. We are hopeful that the data collected will serve to assist all women in educational administration as well as those aspiring to be administrators in the profession.

Appendix B

Follow-up to 1993 Survey, Education's Women Administrators: Their Paths to the Top

Please complete Parts I & II on this page and return with Parts III & IV of the survey:

I. *Demographics*

*Name*_____

*Address (Work)*_____

*(Home)*_____

Telephone Number

*(Work)*_____

*(Home)*_____

*Fax No/s.*_____

*E-Mail No.*_____

II. *Position Information*

*Name of District*_____

*Address*_____

_____

*Position Title*_____

*Years of Service in present position*_____

*Current Annual Salary*_____

Degrees, Institutions, Dates:

_____ _____ _____

_____ _____ _____

_____ _____ _____

_____ _____ _____

*No. of Hours on Job per week*_____

*Age when first in administrative position*_____

*Years of Teaching prior to assuming administrative position*_____

*Level of Teaching*_____

III. Please enclose a copy of your vita or resume.

IV. Your Success Story
            The purpose of our proposed book is to give a few successful women school administrators the opportunity to share your stories of professional achievement with others. We are particularly interested in your personal account of how you made it to a top-level position in education. It is important for you to tell your story in your own style. Please make your story as personal and poignant as possible so that others will be able to identify with and be encouraged by your struggles and triumphs.

            Below are several prompts to assist you in reflecting on your story:

            Chronicle of your path to the top
            Experiences with preparation programs in ed. administration
            Your experiences (as a student) with school in general . . . particularly relating to the
                                                            female's perspective
            Personal and professional landmarks
            Highest and lowest moments or times
            Best and worst experiences
            Sources of strength and motivation
            How women's status has changed since you entered the profession
            Barriers encountered
            Role models, mentors, or sponsors
            Your experiences compared to male counterparts
            Any accommodations or compromises you feel you have had to make because of your
                        gender(personal or professional)
            Strategies to improve communication between the genders
            Specific mentoring strategies
            Personal leadership style . . how acquired? . . how it enhances, impedes job
                                    performance? . . any differences based on gender?
            Advice for women aspiring to educational administration
            Advice for men, women, organizations and political leaders to improve gender
                relations and insure equitable treatment of men and women
            What you would do differently in pursuing your career
            Any regrets
            Future career plans

            These are merely prompts for you to consider; they do not require a direct response. Please include whatever you feel is of interest and significance to your success story. Describe specific incidents in detail to add interest and illustrate your opinions. You may use pen and paper, word processor, or tell your story using a tape. In either case, please begin your account by identifying yourself and your position. Good luck!

            Please return by August 1, 1994, to the following address: